GOD'S LIGHT

GOD'S

A Forensic Psychiatric Physician's Experience
of Creation from God's Light

LIGHT

Dr. Rick Scarnati

TATE PUBLISHING
AND ENTERPRISES, LLC

This book is designed to provide accurate and authoritative information with regard to the subject matter covered. This information is given with the understanding that neither the author nor Tate Publishing, LLC is engaged in rendering legal, professional advice. Since the details of your situation are fact dependent, you should additionally seek the services of a competent professional.

The opinions expressed by the author, herein, are those of the author, and do not necessarily reflect in any way those professional organizations, governmental employers, or academic affiliations of which he is a member nor necessarily those of Tate Publishing, LLC.

Published by Tate Publishing & Enterprises, LLC
127 E. Trade Center Terrace | Mustang, Oklahoma 73064 USA
1.888.361.9473 | www.tatepublishing.com

Tate Publishing is committed to excellence in the publishing industry. The company reflects the philosophy established by the founders, based on Psalm 68:11,
"The Lord gave the word and great was the company of those who published it."

Book design copyright © 2015 by Tate Publishing, LLC. All rights reserved.
Cover design by Jeffrey Doblados
Interior design by Richell Balansag

Published in the United States of America

ISBN: 978-1-68142-936-6
Biography & Autobiography / Religion
15.09.25

To my Shepherd King, Jesus Christ, who made
my impossibilities realities

ACKNOWLEDGMENTS

I express my deepest appreciation to the clinical psychologist for accepting the great challenge and courage to assist me in entering the unknown to discover the unknown. I remain forever indebted to her. In this book, she is listed as Dr. P. because she preferred that I not list her name. I picked the initial *P*, which stands for *psychologist*.

I also express my deepest appreciation to my sister Clarissa (Chris) J. Scarnati-Dull, a registered nurse, who offered emotional support and functioned as the professional technical observer and recorder for the session. She was also the emergency backup for me, if I had an undesirable physical response. She had been an emergency tech in past years.

To my great team at Tate Publishing & Enterprises, I offer my deepest appreciation.

Thank you, Michelle Cabaral, the production scheduling coordinator who welcomed me into the family of Tate Publishing and did a great job getting things scheduled for me.

Thank you, my acquisitions editor, Charles "Kirk" Callaway, who helped me through the initial process and arranged the service of Spanish translation for my book.

My phenomenal project manager, Julius Rama, was very supportive over the many months we worked together and was my liaison with the creative staff of editors, designers, illustrators, and multimedia to help me realize a dream come true.

My cover designers have been so phenomenally creative to create a "wow" experience for me. Jeffrey Doblados's creation of God's Light was just as "wow" as Kellie Southerland for my Soul Explosion cover.

Thank you, my phenomenally creative illustrator, Roy Ugang, for creating a whole series of "wows."

Contents

INTRODUCTION

I was born in Pittsburgh, Pennsylvania, on December 18, 1940. I am the eldest of ten children.

I wrote about my life history in my autobiographical book Soul Explosion, published by Tate Publishing and Enterprises on September 27, 2011.

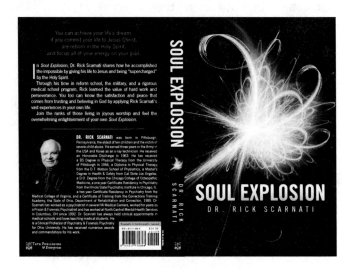

Soul Explosion book cover.

In that book, I had reported on alien encounters, where I had also experienced lost time. This book contains the discoveries of that lost time, in addition to a creation experience.

My Education

I attended Dormont High School in Pittsburgh, Pennsylvania. But in my junior year, I transferred to night school because our home was lost in a fire, and I wanted to obtain employment to assist my family.

I attended Schenley Evening High School, starting in the winter of 1958. During the Day, I worked as a dock worker, loading trailer trucks. On June 1960, I received a high school diploma from the Schenley Evening High School, Pittsburgh, Pennsylvania.

When I joined the army on June 3, 1960, I signed up for the X-ray technician training. After basic training at Fort Knox, Kentucky, I began the army X-ray training. On March 1961, I received a diploma in X-ray technology from the Army Medical Service School, USA Medical Training Center, Fort Sam, Houston, Texas.

I served as an army x-ray tech in army hospitals in the United States and Korea. I was also at the forty-fourth Mobile Army Surgical Hospital (MASH) unit in Osoone, Korea in the First Cavalry Division.

I received an honorable discharge on May 30, 1963.

I then returned to Pittsburgh and entered the University of Pittsburgh.

After I completed my junior year at the University of Pittsburgh, I entered the D. T. Watson School of Physiatrics to begin my education and training in physical therapy. On September 22, 1966, 1 received a diploma in physical therapy from the D. T. Watson School of Physiatrics, Leetsdale, Pennsylvania. This counted as my senior year for the University of Pittsburgh.

On December 20, 1966, 1 received a bachelor's degree in physical therapy from the same university.

After I graduated from Pitt, I decided to go to California. While I was employed full time as a registered physical therapist, I attended night school at California State College at Los Angeles. On June 14, 1969, I received a master of arts degree in health and safety (public health) from California State College at Los Angeles. My QPA was 3.51 out of 4.0.

A year later, I was employed in special education as a registered physical therapist treating physically handicapped children. I attended NIU at night. It was an 80-mile drive each way. From September 1970 to 1971, 1 was enrolled in a doctors program in educational administration at Northern Illinois University (NIU) in DeKalb, Illinois. I was studying for a Credential in Special Education Administration. Even though I had an *A* average, I dropped this program to pursue medicine.

During the summer of 1971, I took graduate courses in mental retardation in special education at Chicago State University, Chicago, Illinois. I wanted to use my summer vacation constructively.

From September 1971 to June 1972, I took undergraduate premedical courses at St. Xavier College and Olive-Harvey Junior College, Chicago, Illinois. During this time, I also studied for the MCAT need for admission to medical school.

From September 1972 to June 1976, I was an osteopathic medical student at the Chicago College of Osteopathic Medicine, Chicago, Illinois. I received the (DO) doctor of osteopathy degree on June 7, 1976. This was the greatest experience of my life. I had now entered the highest of all priesthoods—that of medicine.

On June 30, 1977, 1 received a certificate of training in psychiatry for completing twelve months of residency training in psychiatry at the Illinois State Psychiatric Institute in Chicago, Illinois. Since I did not like the winters in Chicago, I decided to go to a warmer climate in Richmond, Virginia.

On June 30, 1979, 1 received a certificate from the Virginia Commonwealth University Medical College of Virginia, Richmond, Virginia, for completing the requirement of the faculty for graduate medical education as a resident in psychiatry from July 1, 1977, through June 30, 1979.

I had served time in my youth and had given my life to Jesus Christ, whom had helped me achieve impossible goals. I decided I would pay back by becoming a prison and forensic psychiatrist and treat prisoners with mental illness.

I obtained a position with the Ohio Department of Mental Health, Office of Psychiatric Services to Corrections in November of 1979 as a prison and forensic psychiatrist.

Even though I was not required to take the entire training at the corrections academy, I believed it would be a good idea to do so because I believed I would be more acceptable in the correctional environment, and that did prove to be the case. On May 31, 1985, I received a certificate of training from the Corrections Training Academy from the State of Ohio Department of Rehabilitation and Correction. Dates of attendance had been May 13 to May 31, 1985.

My Current Employment

I am a psychiatrist/forensic psychiatrist for the Ohio Department of Mental Health and Addictions. I am assigned at the Twin Valley Behavioral Healthcare (state hospital), where I do emergency admissions to the inpatient wards in 2200 West Broad Street, Columbus, Ohio 43223.

The Ohio Department of Mental Health and Addictions has a contract with the Columbus, Ohio, jails system to provide psychiatric care. I am the Columbus, Ohio, jails psychiatrist/forensic psychiatrist for Franklin County Corrections Center I at 370 S. Front St. Columbus, Ohio, 43215, and Franklin County Corrections Center II, at 2460 Jackson Pike, Columbus, Ohio, 43215.

Psychiatric residents, medical students, nursing students, and others rotate with me at times at the jail to learn about jail psychiatry and correctional mental health.

It is the most challenging position I have had to date. I am the only psychiatrist for the two jails in Columbus, Ohio. I treat as many inmates as I can see when I am at the jails. I receive great assistance from the nurses, counselors, and correctional officers. I could never do as great a job or see as many patients as I do without them. Fortunately, county and state administration are very supportive of our work. I also attend administrative jail meetings so that I may give helpful input and become more aware of problems in the correctional system.

The inmates are sad cases. I still remember my first patient at the Pike jail. She appeared as if she was sixteen. I thought, *What is this child doing in this dungeon?* Actually, she was a lot older than sixteen. When I asked her if she had any children, she replied, "Eight children from eight rapes." What do you think of that for a life? I give my very best for those at the bottom of the barrel!

The jail's medical department has an excellent protocol for inmates coming into the system who are withdrawing on alcohol and or addicting drugs.

I do considerable crisis intervention. I review the inmate's psychiatric record, especially noting hospital and community mental health records, regarding diagnoses and prescription psychotropic medications.

I do crisis intervention psychiatric evaluations to determine what the inmates' mental health complaints are, which includes signs and symptoms of mental illness.

I prescribe psychotropic medications to get their psychiatric symptoms under control as soon as possible.

I also request medical consultations when they also have medical-related complaints that need to be addressed. The jails medical department and I have an excellent working relationship; we do consultations back and forth as the need arises. We want the inmates to have the best possible care while they are incarcerated.

We are very cautious regarding potential inmate suicides. We have holding observation cells where the inmates are placed in the event they become suicidal or homicidal. I always ask each patient if they have any ideas or plans to harm themselves or others every time I see the patient.

Unfortunately, suicides do occur. When they do, I do an in-depth psychiatric evaluation of the case in order to attempt to discover the cause and for any areas that may call for improvement of our system. I also present my findings to jail's Mental Health Administration and our excellent State of Ohio Department of Mental Health and Addictions Twin Valley Behavioral Health medical director for any additional suggestions that he may have regarding the case.

We do everything possible to help prevent suicides.

Since I am also a board-certified forensic psychiatrist, I may also perform forensic psychiatric consultation too.

Certifications, Academic Standing, Memberships, Licenses, Awards, and other Noteworthy Experiences

- Diplomate of the American Board of Psychiatry and Neurology-forensic psychiatry subspecialty;
- clinical professor of psychiatry/forensic psychiatry, OU College of Osteopathic Medicine;
- Distinguished Life Fellow, American Psychiatric Association; and US Army veteran.

I am an active member of all the following organizations:

- American Psychiatric Association
- American Academy of Psychiatry and the Law
- Ohio Psychiatric Physicians Association (counselor, ad hoc committee on forensic issues)
- Ohio Psychiatric Physicians Foundation (OPPF) (member, Development and Public Relations Committee)
- The Psychiatric Society of Central Ohio (president, 2007–2008)
- World Psychiatric Association

- Christian Medical Dental Society
- Physicians for Social Responsibility
- American Osteopathic Association, life member
- American College of Neuropsychiatrists
- Physicians for Human Rights
- Chicago College of Osteopathic Medicine Alumni Association, life member
- VCU-Medical College of Virginia Alumni Association, life member
- Amnesty International USA
- America's Top Psychiatrists, life member
- The Leading Physicians of the World, life member
- Who's Who in Medicine and Healthcare 2011–1012 (8th edition)
- Who's Who in Science and Engineering 2016–2017 (12th Edition)
- Who's Who in America (2015 edition)
- Consultants for Global Programs, board member
- and International Advisory Council, member
- Common Cause
- Mensa (high IQ group)
- Sierra Club, life membership

- Catholic Alumni Club
- Public Citizen
- ACLU
- American Legion
- NAMI, Ohio, psychiatrists
- National Writers Union
- 1199SEIU

I have thirty-nine years experience in psychiatry, prison and forensic psychiatry, veterans administration medical psychiatry, child psychiatry, adolescent psychiatry, geriatric psychiatry, research psychiatry, inpatient and outpatient psychiatry, and community psychiatry.

I have numerous professional publications and award-winning service in psychiatry, writing awards for my book *Soul Explosion*, weightlifting trophies for the bench press, seven active state physician licenses—Pennsylvania, Maryland, Ohio, Indiana, Texas, Florida, and Virginia and a registered physical therapy license in California. I am also an award-winning poet.

I am sharing my poems with you in the next section of this book.

POEMS

AMELIA EARHART: LOST SWAN

The angels did say, Oh Master, create for us a bird of
pure delight,
And God's breath did create
a baby swan's courage to emulate.
One day at play, baby swan alighted on a sleigh,
down a long dark tunnel ride on her slide,
descending upon a colored ball of clay
on which she set out to play,
Missing her, the angels cried fitfully
that God raised a question compassionately,
baby swan, where art thou?
She perched upon a Kansas tree
full of glee
far from heaven's gate
to experience our mortal state.
What joy she brought by her magical flight,
and animals did delight—
dogs barked, hens squawked
as flights of fancy she did embark.

Foreign lands she did visit
with flights exquisite.
Flights of courage brought awe
to all.
Crossing the sea
as night stars beckoned thee,
her destiny
heaven's star,
Angels her loss bewailed, setting off deadly hail,
Struggling in the air, beware of horrid thunder there,
Lightning plunged her into the sea,
opening ocean depths, death's destiny.
A vast dark tunnel opened there
A speck of light beckoned her,
flutter of angels guiding her through the air.
She flew through heaven's gate,
creating such a happy state.
Awe from angels as they saw,
her graceful, courageous flight above them all.
With a twinkle in her eye
brought forth a joyful sigh.
For here, forever, she will fly.

MARY MAGDALENE

Black raven hair, dancing eyes,
aggressive shrieks, rumble, trouble,
What man approaches with entourage? My eyes capturing his
A command, "Spirits be gone!"
Ah! Such lightness! Floating spirit
Oh, what prince before me! Clinging, heart-beating, joy!
Camaraderie with his goal
Mission closing, separation warning, agonizing grief,
Cannot part, he's my heart
A part of him will I take to endure this earthly state
Fair night has come, my charms he will incorporate,
Ripping clothes, hearts embrace, opens flower bud encased
Horrific message, prince taken, life shaken
Whipping, blood dripping, tears falling, heart breaking,
Nails impaling, moans wailing,
Nightmare darkness, earth shaking, death taking
Burial rite, stone rolled closed
Ghastly surreal, three days close
To the tomb go I, empty, anxious distress

A blazing light, my prince. "Do not cling to me," I hear, as my heart envelopes him.
Instructions given, I gather scattered apostles, many goals
My prince gone again
Angelic child healing my heart as years past
My aging eyes grow dim. What blazing light opens them.
Prince before me, arms outstretched, "Mary, come with me to paradise!"

JESUS

Love infused in humanness
A glowing star, address
What low place this straw and dung, fit for the lowest
Servant be you
The word of wonder
Questions ensue
Blind eye, blinking at light,
Sound piercing deaf ear
Immobile, arising
Death to life
A sorrow vigil alone
Hand reaching for calamity's cup as angels tears fall
Thorns piercing, flesh ripping, nails impaling
Ignoble tree bearing thee
Death dungeon slide
Light arising
Maiden searching
All reaching
My eternal song

I received a gold medal for this poem.

Dear Richard,

Congratulations! It is my pleasure to inform you that you have been awarded a First Place Gold Medal Prize for International Who's Who in Poetry Best Poets and Poems of 2011 International Open Amateur Poetry Contest! Your First Place Gold Medal Prize will be mailed to you this week.

It is truly a pleasure to work with fine poets like yourself, thank you very much for your participation!

We would also like to feature your poem and photo on our website. Please email your photo as soon as possible to amy@importantpoets.com.

You should be genuinely proud of your accomplishment! Your poetic artistry will serve as an inspiration for other poets that will follow in your footsteps.

Please keep writing and please stay in touch!

Poetically Yours,

Amy
International Who's Who in Poetry
[Jesus Poem]

MARY

Fairest faun, transformed swan
Coal-black hair, sky-blue eves, rose-petal lips, lightness of being
Gabriel's light sparkles my sight
Fair one, behold our plight.
Will you bear our child of light, who'll give mankind
spiritual sight to enter eternal light?
Will you accept the Holy Spirit of fire to fulfill God's desire?
Gabriel, God's desire does me inspire to which I aspire.
Mary, the most beautiful sound ever heard, you shall name
the WORD, Jesus.
To my utter joy, a heavenly essence grows within me.
Joseph, the glorious star points the way to the place where
we shall stay.
What a joy! My darling baby boy!
Three kings followed the star with gifts to celebrate
from afar.
Jesus' temple presentation led to Simeon's glorification.
Child lost, horrific anxiety ensues, Mary learns of Jesus'
Father's dues

Jesus' band of brothers, traveling to inspire and save others
Son taken, heart breaking, suffering awakening
Passion's surreal nightmare envelopes me as I enter agony's dark sea.
No longer able to cry, I wish to die.
Resurrection light, restores my sight.
Jesus my son is forever risen from this earthly prison.
Mary Magdalene, my and Jesus's companion, bring joyous abandon.
Jesus's brothers infusion of Holy Spirit Fire, possess mighty light to inspire.
Jesus fulfilled communion returns to Trinity union.
With her guardian Saint John, Mary lives on, on Mount Nightingale, awaiting Gabriel.
On a starry night, Gabriel and angels take flight and carry Mary to eternal light.

Holy Spirit

Holy Spirit, third of three, I welcome Your Majesty.
Remain in me, and I in thee, for all eternity.
You and Mary in sacred union, created for us most holy communion,
Body and blood of Jesus, created from sacrificial love, enabling us to achieve heaven above
While John baptized Jesus out of love, you descended on Jesus as a dove,
announcing to him how pleased you are with all his progress thus far.
To you, may this be known, how deep my love for Jesus has grown.
I will forever serve him at his throne.
Holy Spirit of truth, as you are aware, Jesus after Resurrection to his disciples declare,
As I breath on you, know this to be true: the Holy Spirit will renew all of you.
To save others is your due, making all my dreams come true.
Highest wisdom entity, from union Trinity, I beg of thee,

descend on me a tongue of fire, wisdom to inspire,
as in the apostles, to complete your heavenly desire.
Holiest Paraclete, infuse in us Jesus' teachings to complete.
May the fruits of your Spirit give me great power, fulfilling
your desire.
Love so fine as found in the divine.
Mary's joy at first sight of Jesus, her new baby boy
My eternal debt to you for the joyous realization,
I will spend forever with you in heaven's civilization.
May I never cease being dominated by peace.
You made endurance mine by my serving time.
Destroy abrasive qualities from my character, enabling me
to be a kindness protector.
In everything for which I've stood, may it prove I've done good?
Spirit of divine persuasion, make faithfulness my equation.
Make me gentle as a lamb, enabling me to be with the great
"i am."
Let not sin in me take its toll. Destroy it with self-control.
I remain forever indebted to you, for all the horrific suffering
my sins put you through,
watching Jesus' passion and death upon a tree, setting us
free for all eternity.
Holy Ghost, you're the most, all along, creating Jesus my
eternal song.
Incarnate holiest love fire, may in my end, be you my
eternal friend.

LUCIFER

Lucifer, once you were the shining one to everyone.
The morning star having risen so far.
Light bringer while all the angels were singing.
But because of your envy and pride, your brightness died.
How could you leave paradise light to live in darkest hell's night,
Taking a third of heaven's crew to live with you in such fright?
As you did deceive, we saw the fall of Adam and Eve.
Jesus died upon a tree to set men free. Did he also die for thee?
On awakening, one night when I was sixteen,
It was as if I was in a nightmarish dream.
When you coalesced from a mist, I learned pure evil does exist.
I looked into your dark eyes, the windows to your soul,
In that split second, I was seeing evil's death toll.
When I screamed, no sound came forth from my mouth,
for I was frozen with fright.
How could your brightness evolve into such a horrific sight?
Since God commands me to love my enemy, would not he?
Is the story of the prodigal son really you with the Holy One?
Is this God's call to you to return anew?

May you be the one returning as did the prodigal son?
Plead your case with the Greatest Host I love most—
Father, Son, and Holy Ghost.
And the third of the angelic crew you took with you,
May they also be made anew?
God's love is so infinite. It has no limit,
May you live within it.
Do not become Revelation's dragon, but instead, join heaven's bandwagon.
If you in total sincerity, regret your sins entirely.
Denounce all sin forevermore. Your brightness, God will restore.
And you shall enter heaven's door once more.
Help us destroy hell, and make all things well.
Let us all join heaven's throng, living in God's eternal song.

BRAIN ARCHITECTURE

The basic divisions of the brain are the forebrain, midbrain, and hindbrain. The hindbrain controls respiration, heart rate, and its cerebellum coordinates movement. The amygdala is closely related to emotions. The hippocampus helps change short-term memories into longer memories.

The midbrain is the uppermost part of the brainstem, which controls reflexes and eye movement. In humans, the largest and most developed area is the forebrain, which includes the cerebrum.

The cerebrum is the largest part of the brain, eighty-five percent by volume. It has folds and wrinkles to increase its surface area.

The corpus callosum connects the right and left brain hemispheres.

Each section of the cerebrum is specialized for specific functions, for example, hearing words, speaking words, seeing words, and thinking about words.

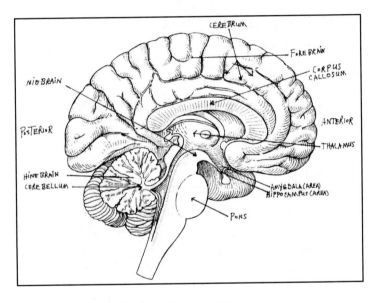

Sagittal Section of Brain.[1]

---

1. Image source:http://pubs.niaaa.nih.gov/publications/arh284/images/
tapert.gif (Author did additional labeling for text content.)

Brain Correlates of Hypnotic Suggestibility

Fortunately, the science involving hypnosis has evolved to such a state that we now have a neural understanding of it as follows:

Structural and Functional Cerebral Correlates of Hypnotic Suggestibility

Abstract

Little is known about the neural bases of hypnotic suggestibility, a cognitive trait referring to the tendency to respond to hypnotic suggestions. In the present magnetic resonance imaging study, we performed regression analyses to assess hypnotic suggestibility-related differences in local gray matter volume, using voxel-based morphometry, and in waking resting state functional connectivity of 10 resting state networks, in 37 healthy women. Hypnotic suggestibility was positively correlated with gray matter volume in portions of the left superior and medial frontal gyri, roughly overlapping with the supplementary and pre-supplementary motor area, and negatively correlated with gray matter volume in the left superior temporal gyrus and insula. In the functional connectivity analysis, hypnotic suggestibility was positively correlated with functional connectivity between medial posterior areas, including bilateral posterior cingulate cortex and precuneus, and both the lateral visual network and the left fronto-parietal network; a positive correlation was also found with functional connectivity between the executive-control network and a right postcentral/parietal area. In contrast, hypnotic suggestibility was negatively correlated with functional connectivity between the right fronto-parietal network and the right lateral thalamus. These findings demonstrate for the first time a correlation between hypnotic suggestibility, the structural features of specific cortical regions, and the functional connectivity during the normal resting state of brain structures involved in imagery and self-monitoring activity.

THE UNCONSCIOUS MIND

Dr. P believes that the unconscious protects us; therefore, she wanted my unconscious to be my guide in the hypnotic time regression session.

In psychoanalysis, *unconscious,*[2] the part of the psychic apparatus that does not ordinarily enter the individual's awareness may be manifested by slips of the tongue, dreams, or neurotic symptoms.

The existence of unconscious mental activities was first elaborated by Sigmund Freud and is now a well-established principle of psychiatry.

The origin of many neurotic symptoms is said to depend on conflicts that have been removed from consciousness by repression and maintained in the unconscious through various defense mechanisms. Recent biopsychological explorations have shed light on the relationship between brain physiology and the levels of consciousness at which people retain memories.

---

2 By permission from Merriam-Webster's Collegiate® Dictionary, 11th Edition ©2014 by Merriam-Webster, Inc. (www.Merriam-Webster.com)

DEFINITION OF HYPNOSIS

Hypnosis[3] is a state that resembles sleep but is induced by a person (the hypnotist) whose suggestions are readily accepted by the subject. The hypnotized individual seems to respond in an uncritical, automatic fashion, ignoring aspects of the environment (e.g., sights, sounds) not pointed out by the hypnotist. Even the subject's memory and awareness of self may be altered by suggestion, and the effects of the suggestions may be extended (post-hypnotically) into the subject's subsequent waking activity.

The history of hypnotism is as old as that of sorcery and magic. It was popularized in the eighteenth century by Franz Anton Mesmer (as "mesmerism"). He was born May 23, 1734, in Iznang, Swabia and died March 5, 1815, in Meersburg. He was a German physician. After studying medicine at the University of Vienna, he developed his theory of animal magnetism, which held that an invisible

---

3 By permission from Merriam-Webster's Collegiate® Dictionary, 11th edition ©2014 by Merriam-Webster, Inc. (www.Merriam-Webster.com)

fluid in the body acted according to the laws of magnetism, and that disease was caused by obstacles to the free circulation of this fluid.

In Mesmer's view, harmony could be restored by inducing "crises" that were trance states often ending in delirium or convulsions.

In the 1770s, he carried out dramatic demonstrations of his ability to mesmerize his patients using magnetized objects. Accused by Viennese physicians of fraud, he left Austria and settled in Paris (1778), where he also came under fire from the medical establishment.

Though his theories were eventually discredited, his ability to induce trance states in his patients made him the forerunner of the modern use of hypnosis.

Hypnotism was also studied in the nineteenth century by the Scottish surgeon James Braid (1795–1860).

Sigmund Freud relied on it in exploring the unconscious.

Freud was born May 6, 1856, in Freiberg, Moravia, an Austrian empire. He died September 23, 1939, in London, England.

As an Austrian neuropsychologist, he was the founder of psychoanalysis.

Psychoanalysis is a method of treating mental disorders that emphasizes the probing of unconscious mental processes. It is based on the psychoanalytic theory devised by Sigmund Freud in Vienna in the late nineteenth and early twentieth century. It calls for patients to engage in free association of ideas, speaking to therapists about anything that comes to mind.

Dreams and slips of the tongue are examined as a key to the workings of the unconscious mind, and the "work" of therapy is to uncover the tensions existing between the instinctual drive of the Id, the perceptions and actions of the ego, and the censorship imposed by the morality of the superego.

The id is the source of instinctual impulses such as sex and aggression as well as primitive needs that exist at birth. It is entirely nonrational and functions according to the pleasure-pain principle, seeking immediate fulfillment of its impulses whenever possible. Its working processes are completely unconscious in the adult, but it supplies the energy for conscious mental life, and it plays a especially important role in modes of expression that have a nonrational element such as the making of art.

In psychoanalytic theory, the ego is that portion of the psyche experienced as the "self" or "I." It is the part that remembers, evaluates, plans, and in other ways, is responsive to and acts in the surrounding physical and social world.

The ego is not coextensive with either the personality or the body; rather, it serves to integrate these and other aspects of the person, such as memory, imagination, and behavior. It mediates between the id and the superego by building up various defense mechanisms.

In psychoanalytic theory, defense mechanisms are an often unconscious mental process such as repression that makes possible compromise solutions to personal problems or conflicts. The compromise generally involves concealing from oneself internal drives or feelings that threaten to lower self-esteem or provoke anxiety.

The term *defense mechanism* was first used by Sigmund Freud in 1894.

The major defense mechanisms are repression, the process by which unacceptable desires or impulses are excluded from consciousness; reaction formation, a mental or emotional response that represents the opposite of what one really feels; projection, the attribution of one's own ideas, feelings, or attitudes, especially blame, guilt, or sense of responsibility to others; regression, reversion to an earlier mental or behavioral level; denial, the refusal to accept the existence of a painful fact; rationalization, the substitution of rational and creditable motives for the true but threatening ones; and sublimation the diversion of an instinctual desire or impulse from its primitive form to a more socially or culturally acceptable form.

In Freudian psychoanalytic theory, the superego is one of the three aspects of the human personality, along with the id and the ego. The last of the three elements to develop, the superego is the ethical component of the personality, providing the moral standards by which the ego operates. The superego is formed during the first five years of life in response to parental punishment and approval. Children internalize their parents' moral standards as well as those of the surrounding society, and the developing superego serves to control aggressive or other socially unacceptable impulses. Violation of the superego's standards gives rise to feelings of guilt or anxiety.

In psychoanalysis, careful attention is paid to early childhood experiences, especially those with a sexual dimension. The memory of which may have been repressed because of guilt or trauma. Recalling and analyzing these experiences is thought to help free patients from the anxiety and neuroses caused by repression, as well as from more serious illnesses known as psychoses.

Freud was one of the major intellectual figures of the twentieth century. Trained in Vienna as a neurologist, Freud went to Paris in 1885 to study with Jean-Martin Charcot, whose work on hysteria led Freud to conclude that mental disorders might be caused purely by psychological rather than organic factors. Returning to Vienna in 1886, Freud collaborated with the physician Josef Breuer (1842–1925) in further studies on hysteria, resulting in the development of some key psychoanalytic concepts and techniques, including free association, the unconscious, resistance (later defense mechanisms), and neurosis. In 1899, he published *The Interpretation of Dreams* in which he analyzed the complex symbolic processes underlying dream formation. He proposed that dreams are the disguised expression of unconscious wishes. In his controversial *Three Essays on the Theory of Sexuality* (1905), he delineated the complicated stages of psychosexual development (oral, anal, and phallic) and the formation of the Oedipus complex.

During World War I, he wrote papers that clarified his understanding of the relations between the unconscious and conscious portions of the mind and the workings of the id, ego, and superego. Freud eventually applied his psychoanalytic insights to such diverse phenomena as jokes and slips of the tongue, ethnographic data, religion and mythology, and modern civilization. Works of note include *Totem and Taboo* (1913), *Beyond the Pleasure Principle* (1920), *The Future of an Illusion* (1927), and *Civilization and Its Discontents* (1930). Freud fled to England when the Nazis annexed Austria in 1938; he died shortly thereafter. Despite the relentless and often compelling challenges mounted against virtually all of his ideas, both in his lifetime and after, Freud has remained one of the most influential figures in contemporary thought.

Hypnosis eventually came to be recognized in medicine and psychology as useful in helping to calm or anesthetize patients, modify unwanted behaviors, and uncover repressed memories. There remains no generally acceptable explanation for hypnosis, though one prominent theory focuses on the possibility of discrete dissociative states affecting portions of consciousness.

APA POSITION STATEMENT ON HYPNOSIS

I am a distinguished life fellow of the American Psychiatric Association (APA), and the APA had developed a position statement on hypnosis.

> Originally developed by the APA Committee on Therapy and adopted by the APA Council in 1961. This revision was prepared by David Spiegel, MD, and Hebert Spiegel, MD.
>
> Approved by the Board of Trustees, September 2009 and approved by the Assembly 2009.
>
> "Policy documents are approved by the APA Assembly and Board of Trustees...These are... position statements that define APA official policy on specific subjects."
>
> *—APA Operations Manual*

APA Official Actions

Position Statement on Hypnosis

Hypnosis is a specialized psychiatric procedure and as such is an aspect of the doctor-patient relationship. Hypnosis is not in itself a therapy, but rather is a state of aroused, attentive, focal concentration with a relative reduction in peripheral awareness that can be utilized to facilitate a variety of psychotherapeutic interventions. The capacity to experience hypnosis can be spontaneous or it can be activated by a formal induction procedure which taps the inherent neural capacity of the individual. This capacity varies widely but is a stable trait that can be reliably measured. Hypnosis provides an adjunct to research, to diagnosis and to treatment in psychiatric practice. It often shortens the time required for a psychotherapeutic effect.

Randomized clinical trials have shown that interventions employing hypnosis are effective in the treatment of pain, anxiety, stress, cancer surgery, phobias, psychosomatic disorders, nausea and vomiting, and habit control problems such as smoking and weight control. It is also helpful in the management of patients with dissociative and posttraumatic stress disorders.

Since hypnosis is a psychotherapeutic facilitator of a primary treatment strategy, it should be employed by psychiatrists or other health care professionals with appropriate licensure and training. Hypnosis or hypnotic treatment as in any other psychiatric procedure, calls for all examinations necessary to a proper diagnosis and to the formulation of the immediate therapeutic needs of the patient. The technique of induction of the trance state usually can be brief. Long induction ceremonies using a sleep paradigm are misleading.

Although similar dangers attend the improper or inept use of all other aspects of the doctor-patient relationship, the nature of hypnosis renders its inappropriate use particularly hazardous. For hypnosis to be used safely, even for the relief of pain or for sedation, more than a superficial knowledge of the dynamics of human motivation is essential.

Since hypnosis has definite application in the various fields of medicine, physicians have recently shown increasing interest in hypnosis and have turned to psychiatrists for training in hypnosis.

To be adequate for medical purposes, all courses in hypnosis should be given in conjunction with recognized medical teaching institutions or teaching hospitals, under the auspices of the department of psychiatry and in collaboration with those other departments which are similarly interested. Although lectures, demonstrations, seminars, conferences and discussions are helpful, the basic learning experience must derive from closely supervised clinical contact with patients. Since such psychiatrically-centered courses are virtually non-existent, many physicians have enrolled in the inadequate brief courses available, which are taught often by individuals without medical or psychiatric training. These courses have concentrated on prolonged redundant induction ceremonies and have neglected or covered psychodynamics and psychopathology in a superficial or stereotyped fashion.

SUCCESSFUL USE OF HYPNOTIC TIME-REGRESSION IN LEGAL CASES

Hypnotic time regression is not hocus-pocus. As a board certified psychiatrist and forensic psychiatrist, I am well aware of its potential for fact-finding and discovering the unknown. The following cases are representative of its usefulness:

Chowchilla, California Kidnapping Case

On July 15, 1976 kidnappers abducted a school bus driver and the twenty-six children therein. They then buried them in a van.

Part-time bus driver and farmer Ed Ray, secured help from the boys. They stacked the 14 mattresses that were in the van, which enabled the older children, to reach the opening at the top of the truck. It had been covered with a metal lid and weighed down with two 100-pound industrial batteries. After wedging the lid open with a stick, Ray moved the batteries. They then removed the remainder of the debris blocking the entrance.

They emerged after 16 hours being underground, and walked to the guard shack at the entrance to the quarry. The guard alerted the authorities, and the children were all rescued. After medical examinations, all the victims were pronounced in stable condition

After Ray was put under Hypnotic Time Regression, he was able to remember the license plate number of one vehicle which led to the capture of the kidnappers as they attempted to flee to Canada.

A rough draft of the ransom note was found at the house of the owner of the quarry. The owner's son, Frederick Newhall Woods, IV, and two friends, Richard and James Schoenfeld, were found guilty by the court and sentenced to life in prison.

After the children rescue, it was observed that similar circumstances of the abduction corresponded to details in "The Day the Children Vanished," a story written by Hugh Pentecost, published in the 1969 fiction anthology *Alfred Hitchcock's Daring Detectives*. Since a copy of this book was in the Chowchilla public library; authorities theorized that this was the real-life kidnappers' inspiration.

Rock v. Arkansas

483 U.S. 44 (1987), U.S. Supreme Court No. 86-130, Argued March 23, 1987, Decided June 22, 1987

Mrs. Rock was charged with manslaughter for shooting her husband. In order to refresh her memory as to the precise details of the shooting, she twice underwent hypnosis by a trained neuropsychologist. These sessions were tape-recorded. After the hypnosis, she remembered details indicating that her gun was defective and had misfired, which was corroborated by an expert witness' testimony

Despite any unreliability that hypnosis may introduce into testimony, the procedure has been credited as instrumental in obtaining particular types of information. Moreover, hypnotically refreshed testimony is subject to verification by corroborating evidence and other traditional means of assessing accuracy. Inaccuracies can be reduced by procedural safeguards such as the use of tape or video recording.

The evidence may be reliable in an individual case. Here, the expert's corroborated petitioners hypnotically enhanced memories. The trial judge concluded that the tape recordings indicated that the doctor did not suggest responses with leading questions.

Vickie Lorene Rock was charged with manslaughter in the death of her husband, Frank Rock, on July 2, 1983. A dispute had been simmering about Frank's wish to move from the couple's small apartment adjacent to Vickie's beauty parlor to a trailer she owned outside town. That night a fight erupted when Frank refused to let petitioner eat some pizza, and prevented her from leaving the apartment to get something else to eat. When police arrived on the scene, they found Frank on the floor with a bullet wound in his chest. Petitioner urged the officers to help her husband, and cried to a sergeant who took her in charge, "please save him" and "don't let him die." The police removed her from the building because she was upset, and because she interfered with their investigation, by her repeated attempts to use the telephone to call her husband's parents. According to the testimony of one of the investigating officers, petitioner told him that "she stood up to leave the room and [her husband] grabbed her by the throat and choked her and threw her against the wall and…at that time she walked over and picked up the weapon and pointed it toward the floor and he hit her again and she shot him."

Because she could not remember the precise details of the shooting, her attorney suggested that she submit to hypnosis in order to refresh her memory. Petitioner was hypnotized twice by Doctor

Bettye Back, a licensed neuropsychologist with training in the field of hypnosis.

Doctor Back interviewed Mrs. Rock for an hour prior to the first hypnosis session, taking notes on her general history and her recollections of the shooting. Both hypnosis sessions were recorded. She did not relate any new information during either of the sessions, but, after the hypnosis, she was able to remember that, at the time of the incident, she had her thumb on the hammer of the gun, but had not held her finger on the trigger. She also recalled that the gun had discharged when her husband grabbed her arm during the scuffle.

As a result of the details that she was able to remember about the shooting, her counsel arranged for a gun expert to examine the handgun, a single-action Hawes .22 Deputy Marshal. That inspection revealed that the gun was defective and prone to fire, when hit or dropped, without the triggers being pulled.

The question before the Court was whether a criminal defendant's right to testify may be restricted by a state rule that excludes her post hypnosis testimony.

In Arkansas, an accused's testimony is limited to matters that he or she can prove were remembered *before* hypnosis. This rule operates to the detriment of any defendant who undergoes hypnosis, without regard to the reasons for it, the circumstances under which it took place, or any independent verification of the information it produced

In this case, the application of that rule had a significant adverse effect on her ability to testify. It virtually prevented her from describing any of the events that occurred on the day of the shooting, despite corroboration of many of those events by other witnesses. Even more importantly, under the court's rule, she was not permitted to describe the actual shooting except in the words contained in Doctor Back's notes. The expert's description of the gun's tendency to misfire would have taken on greater significance if the jury had heard her testify that she did not have her finger on the trigger, and that the gun went off when her husband hit her arm.

Although the Arkansas court concluded that any testimony that cannot be proved to be the product of prehypnosis memory is unreliable, many courts have eschewed a *per se* rule, and permit the admission of hypnotically refreshed testimony.

Hypnosis by trained physicians or psychologists has been recognized as a valid therapeutic technique since 1958, although there is no generally accepted theory to explain the phenomenon, or even a consensus on a single definition of hypnosis. Council on Scientific Affairs, Scientific Status of Refreshing Recollection by the Use of Hypnosis, 253 J.A.M.A.1918, 1918–1919 (1985) (Council Report). The use of hypnosis in criminal investigations, however, is controversial, and the current medical and legal view of its appropriate role is unsettled.

Responses of individuals to hypnosis vary greatly. The popular belief that hypnosis guarantees the accuracy of recall is, as yet, without established foundation, and, in fact, hypnosis often has no effect at all on memory. The most common response to hypnosis, however, appears to be an increase in both correct and incorrect recollections.

Three general characteristics of hypnosis may lead to the introduction of inaccurate memories: the subject becomes "suggestible," and may try to please the hypnotist with answers the subject thinks will be met with approval; the subject is likely to "confabulate," that is, to fill in details from the imagination in order to make an answer more coherent and complete; and, the subject experiences "memory hardening," which gives him great confidence in both true and false memories, making effective cross-examination more difficult. M. Orne *et al.*, Hypnotically Induced Testimony, in Eyewitness Testimony: Psychological Perspectives 171 (G. Wells & E. Loftus, eds., 1984); Diamond, Inherent Problems in the Use of Pretrial Hypnosis on a Prospective Witness, 68 Calif.L.Rev. 313, 333–342 (1980). Despite the unreliability that hypnosis concededly may introduce, however, the procedure has been credited as instrumental in obtaining investigative leads or identifications that were later confirmed by independent evidence. *People v.*

Hughes, 59 N.Y.2d 523, 533, 453 N.E.2d 484, 488 (1983); R. Udolf, Forensic Hypnosis 11–16 (1983).

The inaccuracies the process introduces can be reduced, although perhaps not eliminated, by the use of procedural safeguards. One set of suggested guidelines calls for hypnosis to be performed only by a psychologist or psychiatrist with special training in its use and who is independent of the investigation. Orne, The Use and Misuse of Hypnosis in Court, 27 Int'l J. Clinical and Experimental Hypnosis 311, 335–336 (1979).

These procedures reduce the possibility that biases will be communicated to the hyper suggestive subject by the hypnotist. Suggestion will be less likely also if the hypnosis is conducted in a neutral setting, with no one present but the hypnotist and the subject. Tape or video recording of all interrogations, before, during, and after hypnosis, can help reveal if leading questions were asked.

Such guidelines do not guarantee the accuracy of the testimony, because they cannot control the subject's own motivations or any tendency to confabulate, but they do provide a means of controlling overt suggestions.

The more traditional means of assessing accuracy of testimony also remain applicable in the case of a previously hypnotized defendant. Certain information recalled as a result of hypnosis may be verified as highly accurate by corroborating evidence. Cross-examination, even in the face of a confident defendant, is an effective tool for revealing inconsistencies. Moreover, a jury can be educated to the risks of hypnosis through expert testimony and cautionary instructions. Indeed, it is probably to a defendant's advantage to establish carefully the extent of his memory prior to hypnosis, in order to minimize the decrease in credibility the procedure might introduce.

In this case, the defective condition of the gun corroborated the details petitioner remembered about the shooting. The tape recordings provided some means to evaluate the hypnosis, and the trial judge concluded that Doctor Back did not suggest responses with leading questions. Those circumstances present an argument for admissibility of petitioner's testimony in this particular case, an argument that must be considered by the trial court. Arkansas' *per se* rule excluding all post hypnosis testimony infringes impermissibly on the right of a defendant to testify on his own behalf

The judgment of the Supreme Court of Arkansas is vacated, and the case is remanded to that court for further proceedings not inconsistent with this opinion.

It is so ordered. Her Hypnotically Time Regressed Memories were accepted as factual evidence.

HYPNOTIC TIME REGRESSION (WITH COMMENTARIES)

The following is a hypnotic time regression state that I was put under by clinical psychologist Dr. P in Cincinnati, on Tuesday, August 19, 2014 for two hours.

In my autobiographical book, *Soul Explosion*, I had mentioned three alien encounters that I had had. In the first one in Wisconsin, there was a significant period of lost time for which I believed I had been abducted by aliens. In the other two encounters, I believed there was more that occurred than what I had recalled, and I wanted to find out what else had taken place. In the last situation, I desired to go back to the time of my birth to recall what I had experienced that was awe-inspiring, which I wished to share with everyone but could not remember what it was.

Dr. P was not certain that it would be possible to reach that far back, especially preverbal to recover that information, but she was willing to try to accomplish all that I desired to accomplish in the sessions.

I may be paraphrasing some of the information that she provided for me because I may not recollect every single word she said.

Since I was fearful of what the aliens might look like, I did not want to reexperience pain or terror. I requested that I be put in a position as an observer only in two of the sessions. She believed it would be much better, if she had my unconscious be the guide through these experiences because she believes that our unconscious mind takes good care of us and would not permit me to experience something in the session that would be terrifying or painful. However, she did not want my unconscious to sensor anything.

She did inform me that memory is imperfect, which I am well aware of as a forensic psychiatrist. Since my unconscious would be my guide, my experience would be a dreamlike state.

Dr. P gave me information on hypnosis and what to expect, and of course, there were no guarantees.

She used quite a few techniques to put me into the deepest hypnotic state possible.

First, she had a number of sounds I could choose. I chose ocean waves because I have lived near the ocean several times and find ocean waves very soothing.

She had me do the eye-roll technique, progressive relaxation, and going down an escalator.

She told me my unconscious mind would take me to a number of doors down a corridor in a cabin and would enable me to open the door that would lead to my past experience.

My sister Chris, a forensic psychiatric nurse, was also present in the session as an observer and recorder. I asked her not to interrupt the session at any time but permit Dr. P to do whatever she needed to do because she was the expert in the hypnosis session. Chris agreed.

I was in a recliner. Dr. P turned the lights down low and requested I keep my eyes closed throughout the entire experience. She informed me we get what we get!

She said, "On the count of one, imagine a dot on top of your head, having your

eyes rolled up, looking at it. "On the count of two, take in a deep breath and hold it. On the count of three, look down. On the count of four, release your breath. Keep your eyes closed because you will feel more comfortable. Move if you feel the urge to feel more comfortable."

She informed me she was now going to give me a stress-management session to enable me to return to a tranquil situation, a beach, if I started to get stressed out at any time during the hypnotic time regression session.

She also gave me four quick stress releasing techniques that I could use at any time during the hypnotic session.

1. The eye-roll technique.

2. Counting one to five, becoming more relaxed each time.

3. Taking a very deep breath and then letting it out.

4. Making a tight fist and progressively relaxing it as I had been instructed to do.

Hypnotic time-regression session begins.

Soft ocean waves are being played throughout the entire two-hour session.

"Roll up your eye balls, looking at the dot on top of your head."

"Take in a deep breath."

"Eyes roll down."

"Release your breath."

"Your body, floating, drifting, relaxing."

"Relaxing all muscles in your body."

"Experiencing a soothing massage all over your body."

"Going down the latter of your spine."

"Entire body limp and relaxed."

"Go to a beautiful tranquil beach."

Beach

"Walk along the shoreline, feeling the sand between your toes."

"There is a lounge chair or long towel on the sand that you are lying on." [I choose the lounge chair].

"It's warm, and you feel the warmth of the sun."

"You hear a gentle ocean breeze rustling through the trees."

"You can smell the salty air."

"You can also smell the suntan lotion that you had already applied all over your body to protect it from the rays of the sun."

"The sand is sparkling as if they were white-like diamonds."

"You hear and see seagulls as they float above against the background of a clear blue sky."

"You are experiencing the harmony of nature."

"Counting one, two, three, four, five as you go into deeper relaxation, sliding down the escalator."

"One, two, three, four, five—very deeply relaxed and enjoying the experience."

"Your unconscious mind knows you and will help you experience your goals."

"Use quickly any of the 4 quick stress-releasing relaxation techniques if you become stressed."

"And the tension will drain out of your body."

"You will become more suggestible at that time."

"You may also want to continue this after the hypnotic session to help release stress."

"You shall sleep more soundly and awake refreshed."

"Your mind will be calmer and settled."

"You will take things in stride."

"Go back to your place of relaxation on the beach."

"Behind is a trail that leads to a cabin."

Cabin Front

Cabin Inside

"The cabin is a metaphor for your unconscious mind."

"In it, you see a mirror and see yourself in the mirror."

"You see a corridor of doors, and your unconscious will take you to the door where you will reexperience the past experience you are seeking to explore in full detail as possible."

It is interesting to note that the cabin was very different than the one I had imagined. I am a life member of the Sierra Club and have been in quite a few cabins over my lifetime. I had imagined a simple log cabin with a plain inside with a few windows. The cabin in the hypnotic session, which represented my unconscious, was spectacular. The outside looked as if it had been shellacked. It shined so much. The inside appeared as a miniature castle. When you walked in the front door, there was a very ornate mantle on the left with a large beautiful oval mirror in front, and the corridor was quite artistic too. I wonder, therefore, if this means that my unconscious is artistic and creative.

The prelude to this first encounter had actually taken place in the late fall in 1969. I am not going to name the person that got me involved in this situation for personal reasons.

It was a Friday night, pitch black, cloud-filled sky, and extremely cold. She rarely got involved in my personal business, but on this night, she informed me of a hayride of singles and insisted that I attend it. That was the last thing I wanted to do that evening. It was too cold. She insisted that I go over and over again. Since I liked her and did not want to disappoint her, I decided I would go. She wrote down directions for me. At the time, there was some snow on the ground. I did not have an SUV then. I believe I had a high-powered Oldsmobile coup. I assumed the hayride was in Appleton, Wisconsin, where I had been living at the time.

In any event, I was driving north on an interstate highway toward Green Bay, Wisconsin. After I had driven about 30 miles outside of Appleton, I was not pleased. I had not found the side road as yet, and I believed the whole trip was a complete waste of my time. I wanted to go back, but I did not want my friend to have hurt feelings. And so, I decided to drive on. Finally, after some time, I did find the side road sign, which was hanging on a pole, appearing as if it might fall off at any minute.

I was now on a dirt road and did not feel comfortable about that, especially since I had an old car.

Again, I was driving for a very long time. Now I was completely in the wilderness. I finally saw the left sign post and turned left. There was nothing there.

As I turned the car around to drive back home, I heard this racket.

I rolled down my window, and they were yelling for me, "Rick."

Off in the distance, I saw two sets of two attached hay wagons. They were very long. I can't remember if they were pulled by horses or tractors. They told me to park my car where I was. There were no other cars there.

I walked to the wagons.

When I reached the wagons, they helped me get up into the wagon. I sat down on the hay. I was very shocked to see they were all wearing heavy plaid shirts. I thought, *Boy, are they hardy! I am freezing in this heavy winter coat, and they are not wearing coats at all.* For some reason, I was not wearing gloves. They all started throwing straw, and we were singing songs, and they taught me the songs as I was singing along with them. We had traveled several miles when I realized my Pitt class ring was missing from my right hand.

I was very upset about it. You can always buy another class ring, but my mother had purchased this for me when I graduated, so it had sentimental value.

When I told them, I had lost my ring. They stopped the wagons. They told me to get out of the wagon because they wanted to look for my ring. I told them I did not want them to do that. I said, "My ring is somewhere out in those fields we had passed, and it would never be found. And since everyone was having fun, I did not want them to stop. They insisted I get out of the wagon. It was pitch black. You could not see anything. I told them, "This is a waste of everybody's time. It's impossible! My ring will not be found."

They found my ring. The last thing I remembered was looking down at my ring. I was so happy they found it. I do not remember anything after that.

The next thing I remember was waking up on Monday, getting ready to go to work. I had two days of missing time.

When I attempted to remember what they looked like, all I can remember is it was if they were all wearing happy face masks.

What I find so incredible, and impossible, is that I am able to remember the entire specific details of that drive—forty-five years later!

I believed all those so-called people in those wagons were aliens. They were aware I would experience some very frightful occurrences, especially in the flying saucer.

I believe the lost ring episode was staged. They knew if I lost something of value, and then recovered it, I would probably have a positive experience. And that was what they wanted me to remember in this alien-abduction scenario.

Hypnotic time-regression session continued.

1. Two-day missing time in Wisconsin: hayride to multiple examinations in flying saucer.

Dr. P: On the count of three, you will arrive at the door you want to enter. One, two, three.

Me: It's dark.

Dr. P: Adding a dimmer switch that you may turn up to see more clearly as you desire. Tell me what you see.

Me: Dark mist. It's outside. I can't describe the smell. Pungent smell. No end to darkness. [Long pause.] I am not leaving the darkness.

Dr. P: Bring up the light a little more. [Pause.] More. [Pause.] And lighter still.

Me: Oh. Like lightning. Not as dark. Flashes of light.

Dr. P: At times, you may need to ask your unconscious mind questions. As you do, choose which finger you will raise for its answer.

I chose right index finger for yes, right little finger for no, and ring finger for unknown.

Dr. P: Ask your unconscious mind if you have gone through the correct door.

I raised my right index finger for yes.

Dr. P: Stay in this place. Focus on lightning flashes. [Pause.] How does that make you feel? [Pause.] Keep going back into the darkness. Ask your unconscious if the darkness came before or after your ring was found on the hayride.

Me: After.

Dr. P: Follow the trail of darkness at the count of three. One, two, three.

Me: Darkness is expanded. Comfortable darkness. I feel like I am floating. Comfortable.

Dr. P: What happened next?

Me: I am supine. I am on something. Feels like the chair I am in. Soft and comforting. I perceive something.

Dr. P: On the count of three, bring them more into focus. One, two, three.

Me: I feel them with me. These long tall things with me. I feel comfortable. I felt one put its hand on my chest. Comforting. [Deep breaths.]

Alien putting right hand on my chest to calm me.

When the alien put its hand on my chest, it had communicated with me telepathically, "Calm." I experienced total relaxation instantly.

The degree of total relaxation that I experienced at that time is a very strong indication that I was under horrific stress, and the procedures the aliens were doing on me may have been extremely painful. Imagine a large inflatable mattress being deflated instantly that would be similar to the degree of relaxation I experienced.

As a psychiatrist, I use very powerful, high-potency psychotropic medications to calm patients when they are in crisis. I wish I had the ability to calm a patient with my hand touch, as well as the alien calmed me.

Me: I saw a flash of light. Big dark eyes look at me.

Dr. P: Is that okay?

Me: Yes. I am in a stationary chair being examined. I want to see the

whole thing (alien). I feel like I am pulsating. It's good. It's comfortable.

The chair I was in just appeared from the right side. It was suspended in air at a 45 degree angle. It appeared as a plane—cheap white plastic chair. While I was in the chair, in a split second, I heard a click, and a tremendous beam of light was shot through my body from overhead, giving my body a tremendous jolt as if hit by a bolt of lightning. It made my body transparent.

Wide beam of light shot through my body,
making me transparent.

Dr. P: Then what?

Me: Putting their hands on me.

Dr. P: What seems to be the purpose of the pulsations? [Unknown.] Then what?

Me: They are able to put their hands inside of me.

In this instance, the hands appeared human, but I could only see the hands and arms of the being. Its hands went into my abdomen, and they were manipulating my organs.

Human-appearing hands going through my abdomen.

Dr. P: Not hurting you?

Me: No.

Dr. P: Then what?

Me: I feel hand on my chest. I want to see them. I am in the mist. I think my eyes are open.

Dr. P: Does it seem like they are examining you?

Me: Yes, it does. Hands on right shoulder and side. I want to see them so bad. I want to bring them into focus.

Dr. P: On the count of three, bring them into focus. One, two, three.

Me: I am in this mist. Mist thinner, thinner, thinner, light clearer and clearer. Oh, mist clears. It's like its eyes are in my mind. I can only see its eyes. This thing is pretty big. Wow! Wow! Oh, I wish I could see it more. It's as if mist is pulsating.

Dr. P: Do you think it may be an energy field?

Me: It might be. I want to see that thing so bad. It's there. It's there! I see parts of it's eyes. They are so big! [Eyes] Are calming. This thing is so big. Wow! I feel like they're with me. So strange. There isn't anything real clear. It may have been like a dark misty dream.

Dr. P: Then what?

Me: It's like there is something there and not there. I feel a pressure now on top of my body. It's very strong. Pressure holding me down.

I assumed that since I had to be held down, painful procedures must have been taken place in my body.

Dr. P: Then what?

Me: There is more than one in there. It is cold metallic. Metallic area. Just metallic. It's not cold. Pressure on my head.

Dr. P: Then what?

Me: It's like nothing now. I can't feel them anyone. I don't want to leave them.

Dr. P: On the count of three—one, two, three.

Me: One that had its hand on me. [Spoke to me telepathically, "We will be together or together."] It feels good. I can see it, its form— so big and long. Its eyes are so big.

Dr. P: One, two, three. You will see it, if you and it wants you to. If there is anything more?

Me: It put its hand on my right wrist to calm me. It's silver. It's beautiful, so beautiful. It had it hands on my wrists and hands. I don't think there is anything more. I wanted to know everything that happened. I think I will only remember this interaction. That's it! There is nothing more important here than the interaction we experienced.

Alien in front of me putting its hands over my hands and wrists, communicating with me telepathically while I am sitting in a large white plastic-looking chair at a 45-degree angle.

There were a number of aliens in that saucer with me—three that I was aware of and possibly more. The very tall alien that telepathically communicated with me was fascinating. It had thin silver-appearing body with very long, thin tubular arms and legs and fingers. Its large black eyes were stunning, appearing as faceted gems. In the end, in the grand scheme of things, it made me aware that we are kin, even though in appearance, we are quite different. I wish I could see it again and have a long discussion with it, but I would prefer to skip the examinations.

Tall alien that communicated with me telepathically.

Flying Saucer like the one I was in.

Encounter on Upper Back Porch of Home in Wisconsin: Fire-Entity Alien

Dr. P: You may now return to the cabin corridor.

Me: I am back here.

Dr. P: Go to the door. Behind which is that beautiful fire figure you want to see again.

I had seen this entity when I was living in Appleton, Wisconsin, as I had mentioned in page 93 of my book *Soul Explosion*. It was the same night I resigned my membership in the Bahai Faith. I could not accept their teaching that Jesus is a prophet only. I believe that Jesus is God and, therefore, higher than the prophets, although Jesus was also a prophet too.

That same night, I had an extraordinary experience. I was sleeping in my bedroom but awoke and looked to the door window and saw a being of contained fire. I believe it was an alien life form.

I was not fearful but extremely fascinated by it. I got out of bed and went toward it, but it ran off the porch and over the snow toward the forest. It did turn around to see if I was coming after it. It appeared as pure flexible crystal totally filled with flames. It had crystal arms and legs and a large square trunk, two inches thick.

It was the clearest, most beautiful crystal I had ever seen. Even though it did not have a neck or head, it acted as a complete living alien life form.

Fire Alien

I thought about it and went back to bed. As I think about it now, I cannot believe I did that. Today, I would have got dressed as fast as possible and would have gone after it. I am too fascinated with reports of aliens and UFOs to pass up such an encounter like that now. It is possible that it could have been an advanced mobile recorder.

When I had thought about this encounter over the years, I never believed it just ran away as it appeared to have done. I always believed it had interacted with me before it departed. Now in this hypnotic time-regressed session, I also learned that it is not a recorder.

Hypnotic time regression session continued.

Me: I see it.

Dr. P: You are back in the bedroom?

Me: I see the door. I am in the room.

Dr. P:Let yourself fully experience it.

Me: I see burning flames.

Dr. P: Heat coming from it?

Me: No, it's comfortable.

Dr. P: What else do you experience?

Me: I am in the fire. It feels like a spiritual encounter. It's the fire that is spiritual.

Me in lotus position in flames.

Me: Ah, light. I am so light in the fire. I don't feel as if I have a body anymore. I am so light. I feel like I could remain here. It's so serene. I don't see the crystal part of the entity now. I am just in these flames, burning and burning. Its calming. I am in it, not outside.

Dr. P: Take what you need to, to get the most out of the spiritual experience.

Me: It's as if it is giving me strength and endurance.

Dr. P: Anything more you need to get out of that experience? Are you ready to leave that experience?

Me: I could stay in it forever.

When I saw this entity in 1969, I did acknowledge that it could be an advanced mobile recorder, although at the time, I did not believe that, even though it did not have a head or a neck. And I did learn that it is not a recorder but a high spiritual entity. When Dr. N. H., a Muslim, read my book *Soul Explosion* and about this fire entity, he informed me that he knew what it was. He said it was described in the Koran and was a jinni, a fire creature created by God. Since I had seen it, he believed something very significant would happen to me in the future. I am concerned that this entity never identified itself or made me aware of whom or what it was. It may well have been a jinni, and the very significant thing that Dr. H. had predicted may well have been the last encounter that I would experience in this hypnotic time-regression session. Certainly, it was the greatest experience of my life.

Dr. P: You have two other things to experience. Do you want to move on?

Encounter in Cincinnati Apartment with Dimension-Traveler Alien

Me: I want to move on. I am in the cabin corridor.

Sometime between 1985 and 1992, when I lived in a suburb of Cincinnati, Ohio, I saw a disappearing entity in an upstairs bedroom and assumed it had had some kind of interaction with me. I could only see the bottom of the entity. I had no idea what it looked like. I did want to go back to that time and find out what had happened.

Hypnotic time regression session continued.

Dr. P: On the count of three, you will move down the corridor to the door you wish to enter. One, two, three.

Me: I am actually in the room.

Dr. P: Tell me everything you experience, no matter how unrelated it is to you.

Me: It was the lower half of the entity that I had seen in the past.

Dr. P: Can you see it now?

Me: I am seeing a darkness that is very high and moving. I am in this mist again. I don't know why I can't get to this thing.

Dr. P: Experience that hallway to that room again.

Me: I think there is a rug on the floor.

Dr. P: Anything on the wall?

Me: No. It was daytime.

Dr. P: Can you feel yourself again in that experience where you were? On the count of three, you will experience yourself in that space. One, two, three. [Pause.] Move further down the hallway, then turn around and look back. You said you saw it out of the corner of your eye.

Me: Oh, it's different.

Dr. P: What is different?

Me: Somewhat like the others in the saucer.

Actually, this alien was very different. It appeared as a big silver bug with a lot of attachments, or appendages, on its chest. Its interaction with me was very formal as if it was a scientist taking information about me, and no other purpose. The experience was like being in a doctor's office.

Big Silver Bug Like Appearing Alien.

Dr. P: What are you experiencing with this one?

Me: It's almost as if I am in it. It's as if our heads are together. Our foreheads are together. It's extracting thoughts and experiences from me. That's all it did. Just to come to do that; just to know what I was thinking. My forehead was flat with it. A different plane of space with the alien.

Actually, this alien had a pad suspended in the air, which it told me to place my forehead on it, and I believe its forehead was on the other side of the pad. It was extracting my life experiences. My impression of it was that it was a dimension traveler, who obtained information about different species throughout space and produced a library of different species that entities could learn about.

Dr. P: Anything else?

Me: No.

Preverbal Birth Experience from God's Light

Dr. P: You are in the cabin corridor again, and lastly, in this case, you had a memory of something you wanted to share with everyone when you were born. On the count of one, two, three, you will move back to that time. One, two, three. You are on the escalator going deeper and deeper.

[I was traveling down the escalator at a high rate of speed.]

Dr. P: Now you are as light as a feather.

[I was thought, *I have never been this light before.*]

Dr. P: You are going down deeper still, deeper than you have ever gone before.

[It was extraordinary, but I actually went out of my body while still remaining in the hypnotic trance. That of course would be the deepest state anyone would be capable of reaching, being out of body but still under the hypnotic state.]

Me: Oh, there's no door, just light, light...ah...ah...ah...I can't describe it.

God's Light

Dr. P: It feels good?

Me: It's wonderful! I can't describe it. It's greater than the sun. Ah, ah, ah, ah, ah.

Dr. P: You wanted to share it with everybody.

Me: We live in light. That's all it is. Ah. There is nothing else.

There was more to this experience than what I had verbalized. It may appear to be beyond belief. I had been hypnotically time regressed all the way back, back before my birth, back before I was created in my mother's womb, all the way back, to my creation from God's light.

In the end, being so deep beyond hypnosis and out of body while still in the hypnotic state, I was completely taken over by the grandeur of this light, which I knew instantly was the light of God. It appeared a million times brighter than the sun, and yet, I was able to look at it. I wish with all my mind, heart, and soul that I could describe it to everyone. I am completely unable to do so. There are no words in our existence that can adequately describe the light of God.

I went back into the light of God.

Me floating in a lotus position inside the light of God.

I was in absolute bliss. I had no thoughts, worries, pain, or desire. I was completely tranquil and totally and completely at peace. I wanted to remain there forever. I did not want to leave. I decided I was not going to leave.

I thought about my sister Chris who was there to observe my session. I would create extreme grief for her if I did not go back.

Shortly after her marriage, she and her husband were going home after a New Year's Eve party. The weather in the Connecticut mountains was horrible. Their car hit a sheet of ice, and the car went off a cliff. The car was crushed. Her husband was killed instantly. Though badly injured, she crawled out of the car and crawled to a farmhouse. She was taken to a hospital. In later years, she developed ductal breast cancer. All her black hair fell out, her finger nails fell out, and she was in constant pain and misery during radiation and chemotherapy. I was so upset. I went to see her oncologist. I told her I did not want my sister to die in the so-called treatment process, which I considered torture! She informed me she had to continue with the aggressive treatment if we were to kill all the cancer. So as you all can imagine, my sister had some horrific experiences in her life. I was not going to add to that by not returning.

My clinical psychologist had put herself on the line by having me taken back to a preverbal experience, which was dangerous. I am forever indebted to her for not only helping me discover what happened during periods of lost time but also regain my lost memory of an episode, which I wanted to share with the world.

We never expected that I would be taken all the way back to Creation. I believed that if I did not come back, it would be like taking a bucket of liquid shit and pouring it all over her, and I was not about to do this to my psychologist.

And lastly, I am the only Columbus, Ohio, jails psychiatrist. My patients suffer greatly and need my help. I did not want to abandon them.

I now knew we are all created from this light of God.

Even though Adam's body was formed from earth, and Eve was formed from Adam's rib, their souls came from this light. We learned from Genesis 2:7 that man was formed from dust, but he did not become a living soul until God breathed the breath of life into his nostrils. And further, in Ecclesiastes 12:7, we learn that when the dust (us) returns to the earth, our spirit returns to God who created it. Jesus likewise gave up his spirit to God (Luke 23:46) when he died on the cross. After seventy-four years, I am now able to tell everyone we are created from the light of God.

White, black, yellow, red, Christian, Muslim, Hindu, Buddhist, Jewish, all the others, and even atheists, all are created from the light of God.

I came out of God's light aware of this knowledge: we are made in the image of god!

Our bodies are not the image of God, our souls are. Our souls, having been created from God's light, are beautiful beyond description.

God expects us to reflect back his light in everything we do. Live very holy lives!

Because we are created from the light of God, we have unlimited potential. Nothing is impossible for us. All our dreams and aspirations are attainable!

As far as I am aware, I may be the only human to have remembered at birth that I was created from God's light and able to report on it other than the holy ones of God. I assume the angels came from this light too.

How blessed I am to be able to do this. God has been so good to me. We need to be aware that we have been created from the light of God; therefore, we should make every effort in our lives to live a life reflective of God's light.

———◆———

Dr. P: Enjoy it as long as you like. [Long pause.]

Me: Yeah, I am ready (to return).

Dr. P: Move yourself back to the cabin corridor. You are more enlightened about these experiences. Walk down the corridor and out to the beach, and lie down on the beach.

[Dr. P gave me helpful post-hypnotic suggestions such as "you are always in control," and "you will feel very refreshed."]

Dr. P: Five, four, three, two, one. Fully alert.

———◆———

The hypnotic time-regression session was now over. It had lasted almost two hours. I felt like I had only been under for ten or fifteen minutes and was very surprised to learn it was almost two hours.

My sister Chris informed me that I had not moved at all in that period of time. That gives a clue of how deep my hypnotic state was. Actually, because I had been hypnotized before and had practiced self-hypnosis years ago and have been a lifelong meditator, I believe all this enabled me to achieve very deep hypnotic states. Actually, during this session, I had gone so deep I had out-of-body experiences, no longer being aware of my own body, which enabled me to experience the experiences I experienced even more deeply.

Regarding the meditation, I have meditated on Jesus Christ for years. I had reached such a high state in meditation. I experienced squared spikes going completely through both my wrists. As you can imagine, I was blown away by this experience. I had looked down at my wrists to see if they were bleeding because I had hoped I had been given the holy stigmata. I had not, but I do believe it was a spiritual stigmata giving me knowledge that I was getting closer to Jesus Christ. I find it remarkable that when those large spikes went all the way through my wrists, I did not feel any pain.

My reason for wanting to be time regressed at this time in my life was to discover what exactly happened in the Wisconsin hayride experience.

My ability to recall the entire route and all the environmental signs after forty-five years would be considered impossible, and yet I remember it.

Because I had two days of lost time, I knew I probably had an encounter with aliens. Through the hypnotic time regression session, I wanted to be able to discover what the aliens looked like and whether I had been taken to a UFO or an alien base. I was hoping it would be an alien base, because in the hypnosis, I hoped to recall the route to the base. I had planned to go back there to have contact with the aliens. I have a desire that they might be able to fulfill for me.

I am so blessed to have entered the highest of all priesthoods that of medicine. I had a horrific childhood and served time. Two days before my sixteenth birthday, I was released. The court psychologist had tested me and informed me I did not have the ability to complete high school. I had a seventh-grade education at that time.

I hated authority with all my heart. I read scripture to enable me to find its flaws so that I could even denounce God. In the end, I found my Shepherd, Jesus Christ. I offered him my mind, my heart, and my soul, and offered to serve him forever. He told me in my heart, "I will lead you to all your dreams." I had no idea what he meant by that or how far he would take me. He supercharged me with the fire of the Holy Spirit, and I attained impossible goals as I reported in my autobiographical book *Soul Explosion*.

I am seventy-four, and I am not going to live forever in this body of mine. I never want to leave medicine! In this world, we have global medical groups such as Doctors Without Borders and the medical ship Project Hope.

I am aware that there are supernovas in space, which are exploding stars. Now it would seem to me that when these stars exploded, the planets connected to the stars were thrown in disarray. There must be tremendous casualties that took place during that time. Now I would imagine that higher life forms would have made medical mercy spaceships eons ago to go to the rescue of those planets.

I assume those medical mercy ships have some wonderful doctors aboard. I believe that if I was found worthy of becoming a part of that group, I could remain a physician forever.

I assume that I would need to attend space medical school, and I have a very high desire to do that, even if the program is a thousand years.

I also assume that the aliens would need to clone an alien body and transfer my essence into it, if that were possible. I do not expect that my human body would last very long in long periods in space.

In any event, I wanted to meet with the aliens to discover if my wishes could become realities. I also decided on the hypnotic time regression session because I had made a terrific effort last year to contact aliens, and unfortunately, I failed in the attempt.

I had driven from Columbus, Ohio, to the American Psychiatric Association Conference in San Francisco, California, for continuing medical education courses, and I was going to receive a Distinguished Life Fellowship mediation. Since I would be driving through much wilderness over four weeks, I had very high hopes I would make alien contact.

I used meditation and other techniques but was unsuccessful. At one time in the Oregon mountains very late at night, I felt that I had made contact with an alien. Physically, I felt its initial reaction as being puzzled about the contact, until it realized what it was about. It decided it did not want to be bothered. That was a disappointment. Now I realize that that may not have happened, but I was in such a psychic meditative state at the time I do believe it happened. I was so hopeful of making alien contact at that time that I sent out the following letter to all my close friends:

> To family, friends, colleagues, and enemies (if I have any), As you all may be aware, I am going to San Francisco, California, for the American Psychiatric Association annual meeting.

I will be there a week, getting continuing medical education.

I am also highly blessed to be receiving a Distinguished Life Fellow medallion during that time.

The clinic has been so kind to permit me to take five weeks off.

I will take two weeks driving to California and two weeks on return. During that time, I plan to visit friends that I have not seen for many years.

During this time, I have a major project to complete.

I am highly hopeful that I will make contact with aliens.

My interest in aliens has been lifelong.

As I reported in my book *Soul Explosion*, I saw a flying saucer as a child and, years later, had alien contact.

I am an admitted *The X-Files* addict. Scully and Mulder are my favorites!

The Vatican has had an ongoing alien contact program for years. Jesuit priests have been busy at the Mount Graham International Observatory in Arizona, searching space for alien life. Being a good Catholic, I hope to jump-start the search.

The last time I attempted contact was when I was in the White Mountains in New Hampshire. I was on the same highway where Betty and Barney Hill were picked up by aliens. Their abduction was adapted into a best-selling 1966 book *The Interrupted Journey* and the 1975 television movie *The UFO Incident* as you all may be aware.

Unfortunately, at that time, I did not make alien contact.

I have followed the work of psychiatrist John Mack, MD, who was professor of psychiatry at Harvard Medical School. He spent his profession working with people who had been abducted by aliens.

I was very surprised to learn that he had a lot of the same interests that I had over the years (such as psychic power) and various cults [such as EST (Erhard Seminar Training)].

Unfortunately, John was killed in a London tunnel by a drunk driver.

After going through the cases, I am concerned about the reports. Supposedly, the aliens do not like our species. They believe we are very destructive and are toxic to the earth.

In one case, it was reported that someone had asked the alien, "If you're so smart, why don't you help us?" His answer was that a request had to be made for that to happen.

It also appears that for a very long time, they have been creating hybrids, using us. I hope the plan is not to replace us with the hybrids.

Dr. John Mack had been asked if he had ever seen an alien. He replied he had not and did not want to see one because they are "too scary."

I want to make contact in hopes that I can encourage the aliens to help us with our problems, especially to end all wars, controlled climate change, end all natural disasters, and help prevent comets and rogue planets from hitting our solar system. I also hope to work with them if I can be helpful in any way.

The main reason I want to make contact is that I am coming to the end of the road. The most frightening, catastrophic thought for me is to imagine not being a physician. I don't believe in reincarnation, but I do not want to ever be anything but a doctor.

I have been highly blessed to have entered into the highest of all priesthoods, the grandest of all professions that of medicine, and I never ever want to leave it.

It is my hope that I can convince the aliens to send me to interstellar medical school.

I want to be a physician forever! I realize that in order for me to make the trip to the stars, they will probably need to transfer my essence into an alien body. I do not believe I could make such a trip in my human body.

I know it is a shot in the dark, but this time, I hope to do it. I have a creative idea that I hope will work for the contact.

I deeply appreciate having been here for all the wonderful people I have met, the privilege of having made this a better place by my human rights work and, above all, the highest blessing of being a physician.

I will miss you all. I will carry you in my heart forever.

If all goes as planned, and I pray it does, I will be in an alien body, in a flying saucer heading to the interstellar medical school in a galaxy far, far away!

My best wishes forever!

May God bless you now and forever,

Dr. Richard Alfred Scarnati, BS, MA, RPT, DO, DLFAPA

Diplomat of the American Board of Psychiatry and Neurology and Forensic Psychiatry

Subspecialty:
Clinical Professor of psychiatry/forensic psychiatry
OU College of Osteopathic Medicine
Distinguished Life Fellow, American Psychiatric Association
US Army veteran

Member:
American Psychiatric Association
American Academy of Psychiatry and the Law
Ohio Psychiatric Physicians Association (counselor, ad hoc)
Committee on Forensic Issues
Ohio Psychiatric Physicians Foundation (OPPF Development and Public Relations Committee)

The Psychiatric Society of Central Ohio (president, 2007–2008); (president-elect, 2013–2014)

World Psychiatric Association

Christian Medical Dental Society

Physicians for Social Responsibility

American Osteopathic Association, life member

American College of Neuropsychiatrists

Physicians for Human Rights

Chicago College of Osteopathic Medicine Alumni Association, life member

VCU-Medical College of Virginia Alumni Association, life member

Amnesty International USA

America's Top Psychiatrists

The Leading Physicians of the World

Consultants for Global Programs, advisory council member

Common Cause

MENSA

Sierra Club, life membership

Catholic Alumni Club

Public Citizen

ACLU

American Legion

NAMI Ohio psychiatrists

National Writers Union

I am eternally grateful to Dr. P for helping me discover my lost time periods and especially my creation experience, which now had been the greatest experience of my life.

I want all the readers of this book to be fully aware that hypnotic time regression is not a walk in the park! After going through the experience, I was totally convinced it could be extremely dangerous if you did not have a very high professional experience to do the session as I am blessed to have.

Before I got Dr. P, I had spent about a year in Columbus looking for a highly experienced professional to do the time regression on me. Most of the hypnotists had never done anything like this before. The two high academic psychologists I found were interested but thought it would be too dangerous given my state of health, and especially, attempting to go back preverbal was out of the question. The last two I consulted were licensed social workers who had many years of experience with hypnosis, especially using it for relaxation, stress reduction, smoking cessation, and weight loss. Time regression was not their forte.

I especially wanted the last social worker to do the hypnosis for me. She had many years of hypnotic experience and had been recommended to me by the Columbus Medical Association.

She did set up four weekly appointments for me, each on a Friday morning at 10 a.m. and would permit my sister Chris to be present and allow me to record the session. She had never done hypnotic time regression before, and she informed me she was going to contact her professor at the University of California, San Francisco, California, to get his input about it.

During the week of my first scheduled appointment, she called me and cancelled. She had reached her professor, and he informed her that under no circumstances should she do hypnotic time regression on me. He informed her that he believed it was too dangerous for her to attempt to do it for me. I was taken aback. I told her that I felt very comfortable with her. She had considerable experience doing hypnosis. I told her it would be a new area for her, but I had every confidence she would be able to do it, and I would give her all the support I could in accomplishing the goals.

She told me she was scared and did not feel comfortable about doing hypnotic time regression on me and was not going to do it.

After I completed the hypnotic time regression session with Dr. P, a very highly experienced professional clinical psychologist, I realized that if I would have undertaken this attempt with the others I had contacted in Columbus, Ohio, I believe it would have resulted in some disaster, such as not being able to bring me back to this time.

Again, never attempt to go through a hypnotic time-regression session with an inexperienced hypnotist. It's too dangerous!

Relevant Scriptural Passages Regarding the Fire-Entity Alien (with My Commentaries)

And the angel of the LORD appeared unto him in a flame of fire out of the midst of a bush: and he looked, and, behold, the bush burned with fire, and the bush *was* not consumed. [Since God may appear as a flame of fire, is it possible when I was in the flames I was in God? I was not consumed when I was in the fire.] (Exodus 3:2)

And the LORD went before them by day in a pillar of a cloud, to lead them the way; and by night in a pillar of fire, to give them light; to go by day and night. [God can appear as fire.] (Exodus 13:21)

And it came to pass, that in the morning watch the LORD looked unto the host of the Egyptians through the pillar of fire and of the cloud, and troubled the host of the Egyptians. [God's fire can have negative effects on the enemy.] (Exodus 14:24)

And Mount Sinai was altogether on a smoke, because the LORD descended upon it in fire, and the smoke thereof ascended as the smoke of a furnace, and the whole mount quaked greatly. [God travels in fire.] (Exodus 19:18)

And the sight of the glory of the LORD *was* like devouring fire, on the top of the mount in the eyes of the children of Israel. [The people were permitted to see the fire of God too.] (Exodus 24:17)

And Nadab and Abihu, the sons of Aaron, took either of them his censer, and put fire therein, and put incense thereon, and offered strange fire before the LORD, which he commanded them not. And there went out fire from the LORD, and devoured them, and they died before the LORD. [The Lord may use fire to destroy.] (Leviticus 10:1–2)

And Nadab and Abihu died before the LORD, when they offered strange fire before the LORD, in the wilderness of Sinai, and they had no children: and Eleazar and Ithamar ministered in the priest's office in the sight of Aaron their father. [What is "strange fire"?] (Numbers 3:4)

And on the day that the tabernacle was reared up the cloud covered the tabernacle, *namely*, the tent of the testimony: and at evening there was upon the tabernacle as it were the appearance of fire until the morning. So it was always: the cloud covered it *by day*, and the appearance of fire by night. [God appearing as fire] (Numbers 9:15–16)

And *when* the people complained, it displeased the LORD: and the LORD heard *it*; and his anger was kindled; and the fire of the LORD burnt among them, and consumed *them that were* in the uttermost parts of the camp. [God's fire can kill.] (Numbers 11:1)

And there came out a fire from the LORD, and consumed the two hundred and fifty men that offered incense. [God destroys with his fire.] (Numbers 16:35)

And the LORD spake unto you out of the midst of the fire, ye heard the voice of the words, but saw no similitude; only *ye heard* a voice. [The Lord is the fire and may speak from it.] (Deuteronomy 4:12)

For the LORD thy God *is* a consuming fire. [God is a destroyer here.] (Deuteronomy 4:24)

Did *ever* people hear the voice of God speaking out of the midst of the fire, as thou hast heard, and live? [Nothing was said to me when I was in the fire. I get the impression from this that I would have died.] (Deuteronomy 4:33)

Out of heaven he made thee to hear his voice, that he might instruct thee: and upon earth he shewed thee his great fire; and thou heardest his words out of the midst of the fire. [God does speak from the fire.] (Deuteronomy 4:36)

The LORD talked with you face to face in the mount out of the midst of the fire. [The Lord speaking to Moses] (Deuteronomy 5:4)

These words the LORD spake unto all your assembly in the mount out of the midst of the fire, of the cloud, and of the thick darkness, with a great voice: and he added no more. And he wrote them in two tables of stone, and delivered them unto me. [God performing physical action from the fire.] (Deuteronomy 5:22)

And ye said, Behold, the LORD our God hath shewed us his glory and his greatness, and we have heard his voice out of the midst of the fire: we have seen this day that God doth talk with man, and he liveth. [No one spoke with me in the flames, although I was having a spiritual encounter, gaining strength, and endurance.] (Deuteronomy 5:24)

And the LORD delivered unto me two tables of stone written with the finger of God; and on them *was written* according to all the words, which the LORD spake with you in the mount out of the midst of the fire in the day of the assembly. [The Lord was in the mist of the fire.] (Deuteronomy 9:10)

So I turned and came down from the mount, and the mount burned with fire: and the two tables of the covenant *were* in my two hands. [Such a large fire must have produced awe in all who witnessed it.] (Deuteronomy 9:15)

And he said, I will hide my face from them, I will see what their end [shall be]: for they [are] a very forward generation, children in whom [is] no faith. They have moved me to jealousy with [that which is] not God; they have provoked me to anger with their vanities: and I will move them to jealousy with [those which are] not a people; I will provoke them to anger with a foolish nation. For a fire is kindled in mine anger, and shall burn unto the lowest hell, and shall consume the earth with her increase, and set on fire the foundations of the mountains. [Wow! Is this a powerful fire?] (Deuteronomy 32:20–22)

In my distress I called upon the LORD, and cried to my God: and he did hear my voice out of his temple, and my cry [did enter] into his ears. Then the earth shook and trembled; the foundations of heaven moved and shook, because he was wroth. There went up a smoke out of his nostrils, and fire, out of his mouth devoured. [God using Fire from his body.] (2 Samuel 22:7–9)

Then the fire of the LORD fell, and consumed the burnt sacrifice, and the wood, and the stones, and the dust, and licked up the water that *was* in the trench. [The fire of God can destroy anything and everything.] (1 Kings 18:38)

And Elijah answered and said to the captain of fifty, if I *be* a man of God, then let fire come down from heaven, and consume thee and thy fifty. And there came down fire from heaven, and consumed him and his fifty. [Fire is God's weapon.] (2 Kings 1:10)

And it came to pass, as they still went on, and talked, that, behold, *there appeared* a chariot of fire, and horses of fire and parted them both asunder; and Elijah went up by a whirlwind into heaven. [God's fire can function in multiple ways.] (2 Kings 2:11)

And David built there an altar unto the Lord, and offered burnt offerings and peace offerings, and called upon the Lord; and he answered him from heaven by fire upon the altar of burnt offering. [God speaking by fire]. (1 Chronicles 21:26)

And when all the children of Israel saw how they came down and the glory of the Lord upon the house, they bowed themselves with their faces to the ground upon the pavement, and worshipped, and praised the Lord, *saying*, for *he is* good; for his mercy *endureth* forever. [God's fire had a great effect on the people.] (2 Chronicles 7:3)

While he *was* yet speaking, there came also another, and said, the fire of God is fallen from heaven, and hath burned up the sheep, and the servants, and consumed them; and I only am escaped alone to tell thee. [The fire of God may destroy anything and everything.] (Job 1:16)

Who maketh his angels spirits; his ministers a flaming fire. [This most likely refers to the "burning ones," the seraphim. Even though the fire entity never revealed its identity to me, based on this passage, it had to be God's angel's spirits or his ministers, especially since I had a spiritual encounter with it and grew in strength and endurance. And I had also wanted to remain in the flames; the spiritual effect on me had been that great. I am now certain the fire entity with me was not an alien.] (Psalms 104:4)

Is not my word like as a fire? saith the LORD; and like a hammer *that* breaketh the rock in pieces? [God's Fire produces great effects.] (Jeremiah 23:29)

And I looked, and, behold, a whirlwind came out of the north, a great cloud, and a fire infolding itself, and a brightness *was* about it, and out of the midst thereof as the colour of amber, out of the midst of the fire. [The majesty of God] (Ezekiel 1:4)

As for the likeness of the living creatures, their appearance *was* like burning coals of fire, *and* like the appearance of lamps: it went up and down among the living creatures; and the fire was bright, and out of the fire went forth lightning. [The fire entity that I saw may be considered too as a mobile lamp because the crystal shell contained fire in its body.] (Ezekiel 1:13)

Then I beheld, and lo a likeness as the appearance of fire. [I too saw a fire entity.] (Ezekiel 8:2)

I beheld till the thrones were cast down, and the Ancient of days did sit, whose garment *was* white as snow, and the hair of his head like the pure wool: his throne *was like* the fiery flame, *and* his wheels *as* burning fire. [Fire in heaven] (Daniel 7:9)

His body also *was* like the beryl, and his face as the appearance of lightning, and his eyes as lamps of fire, and his arms and his feet like in colour to polished brass, and the voice of his words like the voice of a multitude. [Fire appears to be an integral part of God.] (Daniel 10:6)

I indeed baptize you with water unto repentance: but he that cometh after me is mightier than I, whose shoes I am not worthy to bear: he shall baptize you with the Holy Ghost, and with fire. [This is another very powerful key passage for my experience in the flames where I gained strength and endurance. The fire of God is a very holy thing.] (Matthew 3:11)

But the same day that Lot went out of Sodom it rained fire and brimstone from heaven, and destroyed *them* all. [Again, the destructive force of God's fire.] (Luke 17:29)

For our God *is* a consuming fire. [God is also fire!] (Hebrews 12:29)

And out of the throne proceded lightnings and thunderings and voices: and *there were* seven lamps of fire. burning before the throne, which are the seven Spirits of God. [This is a key passage for me because the fire entity I saw does appear like a mobile lamp, which may have been one of the seven spirits of God.] (Revelation 4:5)

And I saw another mighty angel come down from heaven, clothed with a cloud: and a rainbow *was* upon his head, and his face *was* as it were the sun, and his feet as pillars of fire. [Part of this angel was fire.] (Revelation 10:1)

And he doeth great wonders, so that he maketh fire come down from heaven on the earth in the sight of men. [That is a great wonder.] (Revelation 13:13)

And another angel came out from the altar, which had power over fire. [Most likely this is a Seraph, and I had been in its fire.] (Revelation 14:18)

And I saw as it were a sea of glass mingled with fire; and them that had gotten the victory over the beast, and over his image, and over his mark, *and* over the number of his name, stand on the sea of glass, having the harps of God. [This is another key passage for me. Here, see a sea of glass mingled with fire. The fire entity I saw had a crystal (glass) body shell and fire in its body. Did it come from heaven?] (Revelation 15:2)

And whosoever was not found written in the book of life was cast into the lake of fire. [In the hypnotic time-regression session, when I was with the fire entity, I was in flames, but they were "holy" because I was in a spiritual encounter, gaining strength and endurance. It was so serene I did not want to leave the flames.] (Revelation 20:15)

Jinn

Picture of Jinn

Surah Al-Jinn

Maududi's Commentry (Tafseer) on Surah Al-Jinn [paraphrased by author for descriptive elements of the Jinn].

"Al-Jinn" is the name of this Surah as well as the title of its subject matter, for in it the event of the Jinn's hearing the Qur'an and returning to their people to preach Islam to them, had been related in detail.

The Reality of Jinn

Before one starts the study of this Surah one must clearly know what is the reality of the jinn so as to avoid any possible mental confusion. Many people of the modern times are involved in the misunderstanding that the jinn are not real, but only a figment of the ancient superstition and myths. They have not formed this opinion on the basis that they have known all the realities and truths about the universe and have thus discovered that the jinn do not exist. They cannot claim to possess any such knowledge either. But they have assumed without reason and proof that nothing exists in the universe except what they can see, whereas the sphere of human perceptions as against the vastness of this great universe is not even comparable to a drop of water as against the ocean. Here, the person who thinks that what he does not perceive, does not exist, and what exists must necessarily be perceived, in fact, provides a proof of the narrowness of his own mind. With this mode of thought, not to speak of the jinn, man cannot even accept and acknowledge any reality, which he cannot directly experience and observe, and he cannot even admit the existence of God, to say nothing of admitting any other unseen reality.

Those of the Muslims who have been influenced by modernism, but cannot deny the Qur'an either, have given strange interpretations of the clear statements of the Qur'an about the jinn, Iblis and Satan. They say that this does not refer to any hidden creation, which may have its own independent existence, but it sometimes implies man's own animal forces, which have been called Satan, and sometimes it implies savage and wild mountain tribes, and sometimes the people who used to listen to the Qur'an secretly. But the statements of the Qur'an in this regard are so clear and explicit that these interpretations bear no relevance to them whatever.

The Qur'an frequently mentions the jinn and the men in a manner as to indicate that they are two separate creations. For this, see Al Araf: 38, Hind: 119, Ha Mim As-Sajdah: 25, 29, Ahqaf: 18, Adh Dhariyat: 56, and the entire surah Ar-Rahman, which bears such clear evidence as to leave no room to regard the jinn as a human species.

In Surah Al-Araf: 12, Al Hijr: 26–27 and Ar-Rahman: 14–19, it has been expressly stated that man was created out of clay and jinn out of fire.

In Surah Al Hijr: 27, it has been said that the jinn had been created before man. The same thing is testified by the story of Adam and Iblis, which has been told at seven different places in the Qur'an, and at every place it confirms that Iblis was already there at the creation of man. Moreover, in surah Al-Kahf: 50, it has been stated that Iblis belonged to the jinn.

In surah Al-Araf: 27, it has been stated in clear words that the jinn see the human beings but the human beings do not see them.

In surah Al-Hijr: 16-18, surah As-Saaffat: 6–10 and surah Al-Mulk: 5, it has been said that although the jinn can ascend to the heavens, they cannot exceed a certain limit; if they try to ascend beyond that limit and try to hear what goes on in the heavens, they are not allowed to do so, and if they try to eavesdrop they are driven away by meteorites. By this the belief of the polytheistic Arabs that the jinn possess the knowledge of the unseen, or have access to Divine secrets, has been refuted. The same error has a] so been refuted in Saba: 14.

Al-Baqarah: 30–34 and Al-Kahf: 50 show that Allah has entrusted man with the vicegerency (generation?) of the earth and the men are superior to the jinn. Although the jinn also have been given certain extraordinary powers and abilities an example of which is found in An-Naml 39, yet the animals likewise have been given some powers greater than man, but these are no argument that the animals are superior to man.

The Qur'an also explains that the jinn, like men, are a creation possessed of power and authority, and they, just like them, can choose between obedience and disobedience, faith and disbelief. This is confirmed by the story of Satan and the event of the jinn affirming the faith as found in Surahs Al-Ahqaf and Al-Jinn.

At scores of places in the Qur'an, it has also been stated that Iblis at the very creation of Adam had resolved to misguide mankind, and since then the Satanic jinn have been persistently trying to mislead man, but they do not have the power to overwhelm him and make him do something forcibly. However, they inspire him with evil suggestions, beguile him and make evil seem good to him. For this, see An-Nisa 117–120, Al-Araf: 11–17, Ibrahim: 22, Al-Hijr: 30–42, An-Nahl 98–100, BaniIsrail 61–65.

The Qur'an also tells us that in the pre Islamic ignorance the polytheistic Arabs regarded the jinn as associates of God, worshiped them and thought they were descended from God. For this, see A1-An'am: 100, Saba: 40–41, As Saffat: 158.

From these details, it becomes abundantly clear that the jinn have their own objective existence and are a concealed creation of an entirely different species from man. Because of their mysterious qualities, ignorant people have formed exaggerated notions and concepts about them and their powers, and have even worshiped them, but the Qur'an has explained the whole truth about them, which shows what they are and what they are not.

Because two of my physician colleagues, who are Muslim, believed the fire entity that I had seen years ago was a jinni, I decided to search the literature regarding the jinni.

I did not find the jinni in the Old or New Testament of the Bible but was aware the jinni had been recorded in Islam. I then turned my search about the jinn to Islam because I wanted a balanced presentation in my book. There are some who may still believe that I had an encounter with a jinni, but I do not share that belief.

During the hypnotic time-regression session, where I was in the fire of the "fire entity," I was having a spiritual encounter with it, gaining strength and endurance. I desired to remain in the fire. It's so serene. There is nothing in the above information about the jinni that satisfies me that it was a jinni that I had an spiritual encounter with. I now believe that the fire entity was a seraph (seraphim/ Burning Ones).

SERAPH (SERAPHIM/BURNING ONES)

Picture of a seraph

Andrew Robert Fausset MA, DD, gave an excellent definition for *Seraphim* in *Fausset's Bible Dictionary*.

Seraphim

Isaiah 6:2–3. ("God's attendant angels.") Seraphim (plural) in Numbers 21:6 means the "fiery flying (not winged, but rapidly moving) "serpents" which bit the Israelites; called so from the poisonous inflammation caused by their bites. Burning (from seraph "to burn") zeal, dazzling brightness of appearance (2 Kings 2:11; 2 Kings 6:17; Ezekiel 1:13; Matthew 28:3) and serpent-like rapidity in God's service, always characterize the seraphim. Satan's "serpent" (nachash) form in appearing to man may have some connection with his original form as a seraph (singular) of light. The serpent's head symbolized wisdom in Egypt (2 Kings 18:4). Satan has wisdom, but wisdom not sanctified by the flame of devotion. The seraphim with six wings and one face differ from the cherubim with four wings (in the temple only two) and four faces (Ezekiel 1:5–12); but in Revelation 4:8 the four living creatures (zooa) have each six wings. The "face" and "feet" imply a human form.

Seraphim however may come from sar, "prince" (Daniel 10:13); "with twain he covered his face, and with twain he covered his feet, and with twain He did fly." Two wings alone of the six were kept ready for instant flight in God's service; two veiled their faces as unworthy to look on the holy God or pry into His secret counsels which they fulfilled (Exodus 3:6; Job 4:18; Job 15:15; 1 Kings 19:13). Those in the presence of Eastern monarchs cover the whole of the lower part of their persons (which the "feet" include). Service consists in reverent waiting on, more than in active service for, God. Their antiphonal anthem on the triune God's holiness suggests the keynote of Isaiah's prophecies, "Holy, holy, holy is Jehovah of hosts; the fullness of the whole earth (is) His glory" (Psalm 24:1; Psalm 72:19).

Besides praising God they are secondly the medium of imparting spiritual fire from God to His prophet; when Isaiah laments alike his own and the people's uncleanness of lips, in contrast to the seraphim chanting in alternate responses with pure lips God's praises, and (Isaiah 6:5–7) with a deep sense of the unfitness of his own lips to speak God's message to the people, one of the seraphim flew with a live coal which he took from off the altar of burnt offering in the temple court, the fire on it being that which God at first had kindled (Leviticus 9:24), and laid it upon Isaiah's mouth, saying, "lo, this hath touched thy lips, and thine iniquity is taken away and thy sin purged." Thus he was inaugurated in office, as the disciples were by the tongues of fire resting on them, the sign of their speaking of Jesus in various languages; his unfitness for the office, as well as his personal sin, were removed only by being brought into contact with the sacrificial altar, of which Messiah is the antitype.

131

When my hypnotic time-regression session was over, I had had confusion and questions regarding the fire entity. It had not identified itself to me. I did not believe it was the Holy Spirit, for the Holy Spirit would have identified itself to me as it did with Jesus as he was baptized by John in the river Jordan.

In view of the above information regarding the seraph (seraphim/Burning Ones) and the facts of what I experienced in the fire, namely a spiritual encounter, serenity, receiving strength and endurance, and the fact that I wanted to remain there forever, I am totally convinced that the fire entity I was with was a seraph (seraphim/Burning One).

The keystone passages that give light to the ministering power of the seraph and seraphim are from Mark 1:13–14 where after Jesus fast and temptation from Satan, "Angels ministered unto Jesus." And in Luke 22:42, in which Jesus in the Garden of Olives, accepts the will of God, and further, chapter 22:43, "And there appeared an Angel from heaven, strengthening him."

This key passage also answered a lifelong enigma for me. As a physician, I could never fully understand how Jesus was capable of going through a scourging and also a crucifixion. His blood loss from the scourging would have been so horrific that he would have died then, yet he went on to the cross. My question is answered by the fact that the Seraph strengthened him to enable him to endure catastrophic suffering. I do not believe any mortal could endure what Jesus did, but Jesus through the Seraph's aid, went the extra mile all the way to the cross! One of the reasons I will serve this Shepherd King forever.

All my questions regarding the fire entity were answered, and I am no longer confused regarding the encounter.

I now know the fire entity was not an Alien nor some sort of advanced recorder as I had thought it might have been when I first encountered it in Wisconsin.

Now I am sure the question will arise, since we know from Scripture that the Seraph is a six-winged fire angel. "Did you see a six-winged fire angel?" My answer would be, "No, I did not, but I am totally convinced that I was in its fire. I had seen its fire contained in a mobile crystal container. I do believe it was a seraph in the mobile container because if its fire light was not contained, it would have lit up the entire area it was traveling through, creating attention to itself, which it probably did not want to do."

I must admit that I am blown away with the knowledge that I had a spiritual encounter with a seraph (seraphim/ Burning One). Who am I that I should be so blessed?]

Relevant Scriptural Passages to God's Light (with My Commentaries)

I searched the entire Bible for passages regarding "light," which I believe may hold significance to me experiencing God's light while in hypnotic time regression. The following scriptural passages I believe are relevant:

> And God said, Let there be light: and there was light. [God is Light!] (Genesis 1:3)

> For thou *art* my lamp, O Lord: and the Lord will lighten my darkness. [The irony here is that God had already created him from light.] (2 Samuel 22:29)

> The Jews had light, and gladness, and joy, and honour. [We all have light, and if we reflect it, we too may expect gladness, joy, and honor.] (Esther 8:16)

> *Why is Light given* to a man whose way is hid, and whom God hath hedged in? [This is a powerful key passage for it shows God gave man light (soul), the

same light we are all created from. God's ultimate goal may not always be apparent, but Job remained true to the light by continuing to reflect his light even under dire circumstances.] (Job 3:23)

Yeah, the light of the wicked shall be put out, and the spark of his fire shall not shine. [This does point out the fact that the wicked started out as light but never reflected it as they were expected to do.] (Job 18:5)

Thou shalt also decree a thing, and it shall be established unto thee: and the light shall shine upon thy ways. [Our light being reflected in achieved goals.] (Job 22:28)

They are of those that rebel against the light; they know not the ways thereof, nor abide in the paths thereof. [Unfortunately, this has been going on throughout history. As we are all well aware, not everyone wants to obey the will of God, thereby reflecting His light that was given to us.] (Job 24:13)

The murderer rising with the light killeth the poor and needy, and in the night is as a thief. The eye also of the adulterer waiteth for the twilight, saying, No eye shall see me: and disguiseth *his* face. In the dark they dig through houses, *which* they had marked for themselves in the daytime: they know not the light. [Evil ones who do not reflect God's light in their actions] (Job 24:14–16)

For thou wilt light my candle: the LORD my God will enlighten my darkness. [The light has always been there since your creation. Offer your life to God, and your light reflections will destroy the darkness.] (Psalms 18:28)

(*A Psalm* of David.) The LORD *is* my light and my salvation; whom shall I fear? The LORD *is* the strength of my life; of whom shall I be afraid? [A beautiful verse for all of us for all time. Another powerful key passage in that the lord is most certainly our light. We were created from God's light.] (Psalms 27:1)

How excellent [is] thy loving kindness, O God! Therefore the children of men put their trust under the shadow of thy wings. They shall be abundantly satisfied with the fatness of thy house; and thou shalt make them drink of the river of thy pleasures. For with thee [is] the fountain of life: in thy light shall we see light. [How true! And repeating for emphasis, "In thy light shall we see light," we were created from God's light, and we shall see the light as we reflect God's light.] (Psalms 36:7–9)

Delight thyself also in the LORD; and he shall give thee the desires of thine heart. Commit thy way unto the LORD; trust also in him; and he shall bring [it] to pass. And he shall bring forth thy righteousness as the light [An example of our perfect reflection of

God's light]. God will help us achieve our goals and dreams. (Psalms 37:4–6)

O send out thy light and thy truth: let them lead me; let them bring me unto thy holy hill, and to thy tabernacles. [Yes, by fervent prayer, we will become greater reflectors of God's light.] (Psalms 43:3)

Light is sown for the righteous. [By reflecting God's light, positive effects are taking place.] (Psalms 97:11)

His seed shall be mighty upon earth: the generation of the upright shall be blessed. Wealth and riches [shall be] in his house: and his righteousness endureth forever. Unto the upright there ariseth light in the darkness: [he is] gracious, and full of compassion, and righteous. [an excellent example of man's God given reflected light] (Psalms 112:2–4)

Thy word *is* a lamp unto my feet, and a light unto my path. [By obeying the word of God, we become a greater reflector of God's light.] (Psalms 119:105)

The entrance of thy words giveth light; it giveth understanding unto the simple. [God is love. He created us all from His Light, and His desire is that we all benefit from the light]. (Psalms 119:130)

But the path of the just *is* as the shining light, that shineth more and more unto the perfect day.

[There is no limit to the amount of God's light we are capable of emitting through our just actions.] (Proverbs 4:18)

There is that maketh himself rich, yet [hath] nothing: [there is] that maketh himself poor, yet [hath] great riches. [The righteous will find happiness by reflecting God's light.] (Proverbs 13:7–9)

Ye are the light of the world. A city that is set on a hill cannot be hid. Neither do men light a candle, and put it under a bushel, but on a candlestick; and it giveth light unto all that are in the house. Let your light so shine before men, that they may see your good works, and glorify your Father which is in heaven. [A very powerful key passage, repeated for emphasis, "Ye are the light of the world." Yes, I experienced creation from god's light as has everyone else! Jesus expects us to reflect God's light from which we were created.] (Matthew 5:14–16)

The Light of the body is the eye: therefore when thine eye is single, thy whole body also is full of light; but when *thine eye* is evil, thy body also *is* full of darkness. Take heed therefore that the light which is in thee be not darkness. If thy whole body therefore *be* full of light, having no part dark, the whole shall be full of light, as when the bright shining of a candle doth give thee light. [A very powerful passage part repeated for emphasis: "The light that is within thee." That light is again our light from which we received when we were created from god's light. We have a grave responsibility for reflecting God's light that is within us.] (Luke 11:34–35)

As long as I am in the world, I am the light of the world. [This is a foundation-stone passage. Jesus is so grand He lit up the whole world with His Light. If we believe that we are true followers of Jesus, we too are expected to be lights of the world by reflecting God's light within us.] (John 9:5)

The night is far spent, the day is at hand: let us therefore cast off the works of darkness, and let us put on the armour of light. [If you have not been reflecting the light of God, you better get started. Time is at hand, and the end is coming.] (Romans 13:12)

For ye were sometimes darkness, but now *are ye* light in the Lord: walk as children of light. [We are expected to reflect God's light.] (Ephesians 5:8)

Ye are all the children of light, and the children of the day: we are not of the night, nor of darkness. [A key passage. We all are the children of God's light from which we were created!] (1 Thessalonians 5:5)

But if we walk in the light, as he is in the light, we have fellowship one with another, and the blood of Jesus Christ his Son cleanseth us from all sin. [We were all created from the light of God and, therefore, should be living in peace with one another.] (1 John 1:7)

Again, a new commandment I write unto you, which thing is true in him and in you: because the darkness is past, and the true light now shineth. He that saith he is in the light, and hateth his brother, is in darkness even until now. He that loveth his brother abideth in the light, and there is none occasion of stumbling in him. [Our light cannot shine if we hate our brother! God is love. Our light must always reflect God's love.] (1 John 2:8–10)

And there shall be no more curse: but the throne of God and of the Lamb shall be in it; and his servants shall serve him: And they shall see his face; and his name [shall be] in their foreheads. And there shall be no night there; and they need no candle, neither light of the sun; for the Lord God giveth them light: and they shall reign for ever and ever. [It we have offered our lives to God and reflect God's light all the days of our lives, we will enter the gate that leads to the path of life and remain with God forever.] (Revelation 22:3–5)

Love Is the Foundation for Reflecting God's Light

Since God is love, if we are to reflect god's light, then we should live a life of love. We find the complete definition of love (charity) in 1 Corinthians 13:1–13.

> Though I speak with the tongues of men and of angels, and have not charity, I am become *as* sounding brass, or a tinkling cymbal.

> And though I have *the gift of* prophecy, and understand all mysteries, and all knowledge; and though I have all faith, so that I could remove mountains, and have not charity, I am nothing.

> And though I bestow all my goods to feed *the poor*, and though I give my body to be burned, and have not charity, it profiteth me nothing.

> Charity suffereth long, *and* is kind; charity envieth not; charity vaunteth not itself, is not puffed up,

Doth not behave itself unseemly, seeketh not her own, is not easily provoked, thinketh no evil;

Rejoiceth not in iniquity, but rejoiceth in the truth;

Beareth all things, believeth all things, hopeth all things, endureth all things.

Charity never faileth: but whether *there be* prophecies, they shall fail; whether *there be* tongues, they shall cease; whether *there be* knowledge, it shall vanish away.

For we know in part, and we prophesy in part, but when that which is perfect is come, then that which is in part shall be done away.

When I was a child, I spake as a child, I understood as a child, I thought as a child: but when I became a man, put away childish things.

For now we see through a glass, darkly; but then face to face: now I know in part; but then shall I know even as I am also known.

And now abideth faith, hope, charity, these three; but the greatest of these *is* charity.

Paraphrasing the above, we come up with:

- Love is always patient.
- Love is kind.

- Love is never jealous.
- Love is never boastful.
- Love is never conceited.
- Love is never rude.
- Love is never selfish.
- Love doesn't take offense.
- Love is not resentful.
- Love takes no pleasure in other people's sins.
- Love delights in the truth.
- Love is ready to excuse.
- Love always trusts.
- Love always hopes.
- Love endures whatever comes.
- Love will never end.

In short, there are three things that last: faith, hope, and love, and the greatest of these is love. Love is the supreme principle in Christianity. To enter life, God expects us to live a life of love. Years ago, I made myself a three-by-five card on 1 Corinthians chapter 13 verses 1 to 13. Everywhere, you see the word *love*, substitute your name. For example, my card is the following, and where my name is, plug in yours.

Rick is patient.
Rick is kind.
Rick envies no one.
Rick is never boastful.
Rick is never conceited.
Rick is never rude.
Rick is never selfish.
Rick is not quick to take offense.
Rick keeps no score of wrongs.
Rick does not gloat over other men's sins.
Rick delights in the truth.
Rick can face anything.
Rick's faith, hope, and endurance has no limit.
Rick will never come to an end.

I read my three-by-five card verses every morning at the start of my day. It is the key to life. Those statements are so simple, and yet so powerful! See if you can accomplish them in a lifetime! This card is the greatest challenge you will ever face. I guarantee it!

The Prayer of St. Francis of Assisi (1181–1226)

This is most certainly is a program of love, reflecting god's light, which I enjoy reading in the morning too.

Lord, make me an instrument of Thy peace;
Where there is hatred, let me sow love;
Where there is injury, pardon;
Where there is doubt, faith;

Where there is despair, hope;
Where there is darkness, light;
And where there is sadness, joy.
O Divine Master,
Grant that I may not so much seek to be consoled
as to console;
to be understood, as to understand;
to be loved, as to love;
for it in giving that we receive,
it is in pardoning that we are pardoned,
and it is in dying that we are born to eternal life.

From God's love comes abundant grace, and what could be more amazing than "Amazing Grace." It is one of the most beautiful songs I ever heard, which warms my heart and elevates my soul.

Amazing Grace

John Newton (1725–1807)
Stanza 6 anon.
Amazing Grace, how sweet the sound,
That saved a wretch like me.
I once was lost but now am found.
Was blind, but now I see.
'Twas Grace that taught my heart to fear.
And Grace, my fears relieved.
How precious did that Grace appear,
the hour I first believed.
Through many dangers, toils and snares

I have already come;
'Tis Grace that brought me safe thus far,
and Grace will lead me home.
The Lord has promised good to me.
His word my hope secures.
He will my shield and portion be,
As long as life endures.
Yea, when this flesh and heart shall fail,
And mortal life shall cease,
I shall possess within the veil,
A life of joy and peace.
When we've been here ten thousand years
Bright shining as the sun. [God's light of which we
are composed will be bright as the sun!]
We've no less days to sing God's praise
Than when we've first begun.
Amazing Grace, how sweet the sound,
That saved a wretch like me.
I once was lost but now am found,
Was blind, but now I see.

OBSERVATIONS AND COMMENTARY REGARDING THE HYPNOTIC TIME REGRESSION BY

Clarissa (Chris) J. Scarnati-Dull, AAS, RN
Associate in Applied Science Degree in Nursing
Northern Virginia Community College-Annandale, Virginia

Observations and recording of hypnotic time-regression session of Dr. Richard (Rick) A. Scarnati on Tuesday, August 19, 2014, given by clinical psychologist, Dr. P.

My brother, Dr. Rick Scarnati, requested that I attend this session administered by Dr. P, clinical psychologist, specifically as a medical professional. I would provide emergency medical attention in the event he experienced any adverse reactions to the suggestions given by the psychologist. I remained alert and attentive throughout the entire session.

The setting took place in Dr. P's office in Cincinnati, Ohio, under the following conditions. The room was lit by natural light through one window only, which was adequate for the three of us to see comfortably. All other lamps were turned off by Dr. P prior to the start of the session. My brother was seated in a recliner, which was in the reclining position. His arms were outstretched on top of the recliner's padded armrests, with his fingers in a loosely gripping position over the front padding. His feet were straight out in a relaxed position, resting on the footrest. Dr. P was sitting at her desk with a note pad, seated at my brother's right side with three to four feet between them. She asked him if he was totally comfortable; he responded in the affirmative.

Dr. P proceeded to instruct my brother on her planned format in the phases of regression during his hypnotic state. She also requested that he respond using one of three simple movements: raising his right index finger, raising his left index finger, or rolling his eyes up to the top of his head in the event he wished to terminate the session. These she asked him to demonstrate for clarity.

Rick proceeded to sit quietly, listening to the voice of Dr. P as she asked him to remember what transpired on the evening of the hayride, his first time regression. He responded with a few monotone words after each question.

There were long periods of unresponsiveness, where I believed he may have either been visualizing so much detail or not seeing anything at all (in his mind's eye). This lasted about thirty minutes until he said he can see huge figures, but they were not clear. At that moment, I was focusing on my brother, watching for any abrupt bodily movements. None were observed. He told us he saw a bright light "brighter than the sun" and continued to give an account of the figures he was seeing. He became very verbal and slowly revealed more detail of what he saw. I felt as though he was experiencing a vision very real to him. He continued with greater detail, and then the psychologist asked him if "they" are hurting him, which he quickly responded, "They don't mean any harm." This first time regression was the longest of the four. I observed a flat facial expression, and no head or body movements, only lip movements. It was as though he was locked in a frozen state. His entire body appeared as a shell, likened to having abandoned it in that comfortable chair.

The second time regression session involved an object he saw in his upstairs back bedroom apartment in Wisconsin. Rick described it as a "fire entity," which housed an alien being. Dr. P asked Rick to retrieve the memory from his unconscious mind of his experience. There occurred many long pauses following each suggestion by the psychologist. Rick then began to describe seeing a cloud. The psychologist asked for more details, Again, there were long pauses. He said he could not see it clearly and referred to it as being surrounded by a fiery glow. After the psychologist had made several attempts by counting from one to three in her suggestions to Rick to bring the object into focus, Rick stated he could see all this fire emanating from an area of the room. He made empathic reference to the fiery object as "the flames" and "its brightness." I observed no quick or jerky movements. His body remained entirely still. In this account, I believe my brother was totally fixated on the entity as he was observing it and might have been too far removed from communicating his thoughts. Verbal responses were very minimal.

As we progressed to the third time regression, Rick experienced and encountered an alien being in his apartment in Cincinnati. With suggestions and prompts from Dr. P, Rick was slow to reveal distinctive details of this vision that was in the process of disappearing upon him entering his bedroom. He responded by saying he was only able to see the bottom part of the entity. The psychologist asked if he could be more descriptive of this object before it vanished. There was a long silence. At this point, I observed no subtle changes in Rick's appearance throughout this entire third time regression. Rick's verbal responses were few.

In the final and fourth time regression, Rick revealed his astonishing and lucid memory of primordial "back to the womb" vision. This is his moment in creation in which he can feel immersed in God's light. When regressing back,

Dr. P asked for details. Rick responded with his seeing a "glorious, brilliant and beautiful white light brighter that the sun." "It's wonderful." "It's so bright." As he observed this light in his mind's eye, his voice was empathic. He then provided no further details and remained motionless until Dr. P brought him back to consciousness.

In conclusion, this was the first session of hypnosis I have witnessed where I was an observer. I have provided my observations and feelings throughout this narrative and found this two-hour session remarkable due to physiological dynamics as I observed the absence of facial expression or flat affect, absence of movement of the head or torso, and absence of involuntary muscular contractions of the extremities. In anyone's mind, for the unconscious mind to delve into material content of this nature, they would surmise it could very possibly trigger increases in blood pressure and pulse, rapid breathing, visual signs of perspiration, along with disturbing cries of fear or elation, screaming, indistinct utterances, or, worse, convulsions, cardiac arrest, or stroke. This type of session might also elicit disturbing projections of the details of the event in the unconscious and cause a violent episode. In my mind, I was prepared for an altogether different outcome from this session. My brother had informed me that he had studied and utilized the art of meditation for many years. Had this capability played any part and had this been the reason there were no superficial or obvious physical reactions/gestures as he went through his time regression.

My final conclusion is based on a number of facts. (1) My brother's purpose in submitting to hypnosis was to uncover the knowledge of the events he witnessed at varying times in his life. He had no ulterior motive than to satisfy his own mind and to find closure; (2) he did extensive and intensive research in finding the most qualified professional. He believed Dr. P to be godsend and believed she was exactly the professional he had hoped to obtain, hoping to satisfy answers to questions that had been locked in his unconscious mind for most of his life; (3) clearly, throughout this session as an observer, I believe that my brother was completely tuned in to his unconscious state. His sensory and motor-neural connections from his conscious mind to his body appeared to be shut down evidenced by the absence of all movements. His senses and heightened awareness seemed to be guided by his unconscious during periods when he did not respond to Dr. P. During those periods of silence, he appeared to be an observer himself of the occurring event as it happened.

Lastly, as a skeptic in this realm of science, I have developed more of an open mind after witnessing this session. My perspective through this enlightening experience would be to acknowledge that the key to understanding and knowledge is unlocking the door to the unknown.

Conclusions and Recommendations

- We all have been created from the light of God.

- White, black, yellow, red, Christian, Muslim, Hindu, Buddhist, Jew, all others, and even atheists, all are created from the light of God.

- We are made in the image of God! Our bodies are not the image of God, our souls are. Our souls, having been created from God's light, are beautiful beyond description.

- Because we are created from the light of God, we have unlimited potential. Nothing is impossible for us. We can attain our dreams and aspirations.

God expects us to reflect his light back in everything we do. In other words, we are expected to live very holy lives!

I am the objective proof that nothing is impossible! I came from a very dysfunctional family. I had suffered tremendous physical abuse as a child.

I served time for years. When I was released two days before my sixteenth birthday, the PhD court psychologist recommended that I learn a trade because the tests showed that I was not capable of completing high school. I had a seventh-grade education at that time.

As a psychiatrist, I can tell all of you without any hesitation whatsoever that given my life situation, there is no way I could have achieved the impossible, but I did. You can too! If you offer your whole mind, heart, and soul to God and work harder that you have ever worked before, you can achieve your "impossible dream" because you have been created from the light of God.

Because we have been created from the light of God, we are expected to live a life that is reflective of God's light.

At the judgment, we will be held accountable regarding how well we reflected God's light in our earthly behavior.

We must always strive to be the best we can be.

In view of the fact that we are all created from the light of God, all of the so-called religious wars we are fighting is complete and utter insanity! God expects us all to work together in peace, not killing each other as we are doing.

It is possible to achieve hypnotic time regression with a highly trained, experienced, empathic professional, but there are risks in entering the unknown.

As I have stated, my heart's desire was to be a physician forever, but after I have experienced God's light, my only desire is to be with God. Now if in heaven we are given a choice of a permanent career, then of course, I will choose medicine.

Travel your journey here with God! You can't lose! It's a win-win situation.

We all are God's light in the world!

May your light always shine brightly!

I hope to meet all of you in God's light.

Picture of Dr. Rick Scarnati

Sources

Richard (Rick) Alfred Scarnati, *Soul Explosion*. OK: Tate Publishing and Enterprises, LLC, 2011).

Rick Scarnati, "Amelia Earhart: Lost Swan." In *Stars in Our Hearts: Notions* (Utah: Word Poetry Movement, 2012), 184–5.

Rick Scarnati, "Mary Magdalene." In *Best Poets and Poems of 2012* (Utah: World Poetry Movement), 279–280.

Richard A. Scarnati, "Jesus." In *International Who's Who in Poetry 2012* (California: International Who's Who), 301.

———◆———

1. The Brain's Inner Workings, A Guide for Students
   National Institute of Mental Health
   Science Writing, Press & Dissemination Branch
   6001. Executive Boulevard
   Room 8184, MSC 9663
   Bethesda, MD 20892–9663

Phone: 301–443–4513 or
Toll-free: 1–866–615–NIMH (6464)
TTY Toll-free: 1–866–415–8051
Fax: 301–443–4279
E-mail: nimhinfo@nih.gov
Website: http://www.nimh.nih.gov

2. Sagittal Section of Brain: Imagesource:http://pubs.niaaa.nih.gov/publications/arh284/images/tapert.gif (Author did additional labeling for text content).

3. National Institute of Health (NIH)/National Institute on Alcohol Abuse and Alcoholism. http://www.niaaa.nih.gov

Citation: Huber A, Lui F, Duzzi D, Pagnoni G, Porro CA (2014) Structural and Functional Cerebral Correlates of Hypnotic Suggestibility. PLoS ONE 9(3): e93187. doi:10.1371/journal.pone.0093187

Editor: Peter W. Halligan, University of Cardiff, United States of America Received: December 9, 2013; Accepted: March 1, 2014; Published: March 26, 2014 Copyright: © 2014 Huber et al. This is an open-access article distributed under the terms of the Creative Commons Attribution License, which permits unrestricted use, distribution, and reproduction in any medium, provided the original author and source are credited. Funding: The authors thank the Fondazione Cassa di Risparmio di Modena

(FCRM) for its financial support to the Modena MR center. A.H. is supported by a FCRM International grant 2010 (code: A0FF-0AAB-9711-FA30).

4. Unconscious mind (UNCONSCIOUS)
   From Merriam-Webster Inc.
   47. Federal St., P.O. Box 281
   Springfield, MA 01102

5. Definition of Hypnosis
   From Merriam-Webster Inc.
   Federal St., P.O. Box 281
   Springfield, MA 01102

6. Jinn
   Aalim On Line
   The Only Quran
   www.theonlyquran.com

PERMISSIONS

1. Section of Brain: Imagesource:http://pubs.niaaa. nih.gov/publications/arh284/images/tapert.gif (Author did additional labeling for text content). National Institute of Health (NIH)/National Institute on Alcohol Abuse and Alcoholism. http:// www.niaaa.nih.gov. Permission obtained, Oct. 20, 2014, Maureen Gardner, NIH/NIAAA.

2. Huber A, Lui F, Duzzi D, Pagnoni G, Porro CA (2014) *Structural and Functional Cerebral Correlates of Hypnotic Suggestibility*. PLoS ONE 9(3): e93187. doi:10.1371/journal.pone.0093187

   Editor: Peter W. Halligan, University of Cardiff, United States of America Received: December 9, 2013; Accepted: March 1, 2014; Published: March 26, 2014

tion in any medium, provided the original author and source are credited.

3. Unconscious mind (Unconscious). By permission. From Merriam-Webster's Collegiate® Dictionary, 11th Edition ©2014 by Merriam-Webster, Inc. (www.Merriam-Webster.com)

4. Definition of Hypnosis. By permission. From Merriam-Webster's Collegiate® Dictionary, 11th Edition ©2014 by Merriam-Webster, Inc. (www.Merriam-Webster.com).

5. APA Position Statement on Hypnosis

   APA Position Statement on Hypnosis. Reproduced with permission from the American Psychiatric Association. Copyright©2009. All Rights Reserved.

6. Picture of alien from Dr. John Mack's website.
   John E. Mack Institute
   PO Box 7046
   Boulder CO 80304
   info@johnemackinstitute.org

   (Picture could not be used because author could not locate owner to obtain permission use.)

7. Jinn
   Permission obtained: Aalim On Line, The Only Quran, www.theonlyquran.com.

8. (MY PHOTO) By Permission from Rick Buchanan
Photography
243. North Fifth St., Suite # 220
Columbus, OH 43215
614. 893-7425
www.rickbuchananphotography.com